MW01157110

The Many Faces of
GEORGE WASHINGTON

REMAKING A PRESIDENTIAL ICON

Carla Killough McClafferty

CAROLRHODA BOOKS · MINNEAPOLIS

FOR MY CHILDREN, RYAN MCCLAFFERTY
AND BRITTNEY MCCLAFFERTY

—C.K.M.

The author gratefully acknowledges two staff members at George Washington's Mount Vernon Estate and Gardens for their expert reading of this manuscript: Ann Bay, vice president for education, and Mary V. Thompson, research historian.

A NOTE ON SPELLING AND USAGE
I have chosen to use exact quotes, complete with eighteenth-century spelling, capitalization, and grammatical usage, wherever possible throughout this text. *The Many Faces of George Washington* is a book about the search for a man as he really was. It seemed only right, then, to include people's words as they really wrote and spoke them—even if those words seem wrong to modern eyes.

Carolrhoda Books
A division of Lerner Publishing Group, Inc.
241 First Avenue North
Minneapolis, MN 55401 U.S.A.

Website address: www.lernerbooks.com

Library of Congress Cataloging-in-Publication Data

McClafferty, Carla Killough, 1958–
    The many faces of George Washington : remaking a presidential icon / By
Carla Killough McClafferty.
        p.   cm.
    Includes bibliographical references and index.
    ISBN: 978-0-7613-5608-0 (lib. bdg. : alk. paper)
    1. Washington, George, 1732–1799—Statues—Juvenile literature.
    2. Washington, George, 1732–1799—Juvenile literature. 3. Presidents—United
States—Biography—Juvenile literature. I. Title.
    E312.66.M13 2011
    973.4'1092—dc22 [B]   2010028178

Manufactured in the United States of America
1 - PC - 12/31/10

CONTENTS

THIS PORTRAIT OF WASHINGTON by Gilbert Stuart, known as the Athenaeum portrait, has appeared on the dollar bill since 1869. Martha Washington commissioned Stuart to paint portraits of her and her husband to hang at Mount Vernon in 1796. The artist was so pleased with the image of the president that he kept it unfinished to use as a reference. Although Martha repeatedly asked Stuart to finish the paintings, he never did. Over the years, Stuart sold approximately seventy-five copies of this portrait.

CHAPTER ONE

SEARCHING FOR GEORGE WASHINGTON

The image most Americans have of George Washington comes from the one-dollar bill, and this is somewhat unfortunate. Gilbert Stuart painted the famous portrait on which the bill's image is based in the spring of 1796. At that time, sixty-four-year-old Washington was in his third year of a challenging second term as president. When Washington sat for the artist, his last tooth had recently been pulled. The upper and lower plates of his new false teeth were held together with a heavy spring that made speaking difficult. The denture was uncomfortable and hard to keep in his mouth. The dignified man was embarrassed by the way it made his lips bulge out. President Washington probably had no idea this painting by Stuart would become the portrait that would define his image for future generations.

But did George Washington really look like Stuart's portrait seen on the dollar bill? According to John Neal, a nineteenth-century art critic, this famous image didn't look like Washington at all. In 1823 he wrote, "Though a better likeness of him were shown to us, we should reject it; for, the only idea that we now have of George Washington, is associated with Stuart's Washington. . . . If Washington should appear on earth, just as he sat to Stuart, I am sure that he would be treated as an imposter, when compared with Stuart's likeness of him, unless he produced his credentials." In truth, Stuart was only one of many artists who painted the likeness of this founding father. Each artist had his own interpretation of Washington and executed that interpretation using his individual skills, strengths, and styles. As a result, each portrait of Washington is unique.

People who had seen Washington in person realized portraits of him didn't quite capture his image. A British visitor, in describing his impressions after meeting Washington in 1790, said, "No picture accurately resembled him in the minute traits of his person.... There was an expression of his face that no painter had succeeded in taking."

Julian Ursyn Niemcewicz, a visitor to Mount Vernon, wrote in his journal on May 21, 1798, about a conversation he'd had with Martha Washington and one of her granddaughters. He wrote that he "spoke with Mrs. Washington of the little likeness there is between the General [George Washington] and his portraits." Niemcewicz also noted that "the portraits that we have of him in Europe do not resemble him much."

An even more striking illustration of the variation among portraits of Washington comes from the work of artists Rembrandt Peale and his father, Charles Willson Peale. George Washington agreed to sit for Rembrandt Peale three times during September 1795. Although the gifted portrait painter was only seventeen years old, he was given a rare opportunity to paint the president of the United States. The day of the first sitting,

AT ANY GIVEN TIME, more than nine billion dollar bills are in circulation around the world, making it the most common image of Washington by far. However, the image of Washington is backward to the way anyone would have seen him. The image of Washington on the dollar is a mirror image of the Athenaeum portrait because the engraving process causes the image to be reversed.

the young artist got up before daybreak to prepare his equipment and mix his paints. He wanted to be ready for President Washington's prompt arrival at seven o'clock. Rembrandt later wrote that he was concerned that "anxiety would overpower me and that I should fail in my purpose." To calm his nerves, his father agreed to paint alongside him. The president had known the elder Peale for a long time. He was the first artist to paint Washington's portrait in 1772, and Charles Willson Peale fought under Washington's command during the American Revolution (1775–1783). With President Washington sitting in front of them, Rembrandt Peale began his work. At Rembrandt's right side, his father also painted while he chatted with Washington. When they were finished, Rembrandt's image showed the sixty-three-year-old president as a tired-looking, older man. His father's portrait showed him as more youthful and serene.

If the portraits painted by the country's leading artists don't give us an accurate image of the man, then how did he really look?

The Mount Vernon Ladies' Association, which owns and maintains George Washington's Mount Vernon Estate and Gardens, and James Rees, the site's president, set up focus groups to assess

REMBRANDT PEALE was seventeen years old when he painted this portrait of President Washington *(above)* in 1795. At the same sitting where Rembrandt Peale painted Washington, his father, Charles Willson Peale, painted this portrait *(below).*

GILBERT STUART painted his first portrait of Washington *(left)* in 1795, about a year before his Athenaeum portrait and around the same time as the portraits done by Rembrandt and Charles Willson Peale. Stuart painted about a dozen copies of this pose, which became known as the Vaughan portrait. A miniature by John Ramage *(center)* was the first painting of Washington after he became president. On October 3, 1789, Washington wrote in his journal that he sat for two hours so a miniature could be made for his wife, Martha. One month later, on November 3, 1789, Washington sat for this portrait by Christian Gullager *(right)*.

the public's knowledge and impressions of Washington. The research revealed two main issues. First, the general public knew fewer facts about George Washington and his role in American history today than the general public did about thirty years ago. Second, when participants were asked what they thought of Washington when they saw the famous Gilbert Stuart portrait, many responded by using words like "stiff," "old," "grumpy," and even "boring."

Their comments surprised Rees, who said, "Boring is not a word anyone in the eighteenth century would have used to describe George Washington. He was the most robust, athletic, outdoorsy, and adventurous of all the founding fathers. He was the 'man of action' of the

THIS MINIATURE OF WASHINGTON *(left)* was painted in 1791 by Archibald Robertson. One year later, Washington refused to sit for painter William Joseph Williams. Washington wrote, "I am so heartily tired of the attendance which, from one cause or another, I have bestowed on these kind of people, that it is now more than two years since I have resolved to sit no more for any of them; and have adhered to it; except in instances where it has been requested by public bodies, or for a particular purpose (not of the painters) and could not, without offence, be refused." Williams then offered to paint the portrait for the Alexandria (Virginia) Lodge No. 22, of which Washington was a member, thus making it impossible for Washington to refuse. The painting *(right)* was finished in 1794.

eighteenth century. The real Washington made heads turn."

The leadership at Mount Vernon knew they must do something to change this impression. An education building was planned to teach visitors to Mount Vernon about Washington's character and leadership abilities. Since Stuart's image gave people the impression that Washington was grumpy and boring, could a more accurate image of the man change that perception? James Rees was determined to find out.

As the plan began to take shape, Rees turned to Ann Bay, vice president for education at Mount Vernon, to serve as the project director. They decided to create three life-sized re-creations of George Washington for the education building. They wanted to show him at three pivotal moments in his life: as a nineteen-year-old surveyor in the American wilderness, as a forty-five-year-old general of the Continental Army at Valley Forge, and as a fifty-seven-year-old president of the United States of America taking the oath of office.

To depict Washington accurately, the leadership of Mount Vernon decided to investigate him in a way that had never been done before. They would gather a team of experts from the fields of science, history, and art to find out as much as possible about Washington's body, clothes, daily life, manners, customs, and work. They would use every tool available, including the latest technology, as they compiled facts about the man.

· · ·

The first expert they brought in was Jeffrey H. Schwartz, a forensic anthropologist at the University of Pittsburgh. When an unidentified skeleton is found, to make an identification, sometimes anthropologists like Schwartz are asked to re-create how that person looked during his or her lifetime. To accomplish this, forensic anthropologists take the skull of the deceased person and using their knowledge of muscles and skin depth, they sculpt the face with clay. The result is a reliable way to reconstruct an unknown person's face. This would have been the easiest place to begin determining what George Washington looked like. But this method was not an option. Not disturbing Washington's body was a requirement of the sales contract between the Washington family and the Mount Vernon Ladies' Association when the association purchased the property in 1858.

When Schwartz learned that Washington's remains were off-limits, he thought, "No bones? How could I begin to imagine doing a forensic reconstruction without bones?"

The fact that Schwartz couldn't approach the project in the traditional way made the search for the real George Washington more challenging—and more intriguing. He would need to gather information from other sources.

Schwartz began the investigation by consulting Ellen G. Miles, curator of painting and sculpture at the Smithsonian National Portrait Gallery. Together they looked at life portraits, those painted while Washington was physically sitting in front of the artist. Most of these were from Washington's presidential years, a few were from the American Revolution period, and no portraits exist of him younger than the age of forty. Washington was the model for each one, but each of them showed a very different-looking man. Did any of these artists paint the "real" George Washington?

Schwartz found that the best evidence did not come from a painted portrait at all, but it did come from an artist: the French sculptor Jean-Antoine Houdon.

CHAPTER TWO

CAPTURING GEORGE WASHINGTON

Capturing Washington's three-dimensional likeness is not a new desire. In 1785 the Virginia state legislature wanted to honor Washington for leading the Continental Army to victory. They planned to place a statue of him in the rotunda of the new state capitol building in Richmond that was being designed by Thomas Jefferson.

Benjamin Franklin and Jefferson agreed that Jean-Antoine Houdon was the artist who should create the statue. Houdon was considered to be the finest sculptor in Europe at that time. From his studio in Paris, France, he had already created busts of many European monarchs and other important people, including Franklin. When Houdon was given the chance to sculpt Washington, he dropped everything to do so—including negotiations to sculpt Catherine the Great, the empress of Russia.

At first Benjamin Harrison, governor of Virginia, suggested that Houdon use a full-length portrait of Washington by Charles Willson Peale as a reference for the statue. But Houdon insisted that a portrait was not enough—he must see George Washington for himself. When all the details were settled, Houdon agreed to a fee of what today would amount to about five thousand dollars. The trip across the Atlantic was much riskier than it is today, so Houdon also received a life insurance policy. The long trip would be worth it to meet Washington face-to-face and preserve his image in marble.

Houdon planned to stay at Mount Vernon for a couple of weeks to get to know George Washington. After Houdon gathered all the information he needed, he would return to his studio in Paris to create the statue.

Houdon left Paris at the end of July 1785. By the time he arrived in Virginia, shades of red, yellow, and orange colored the autumn leaves. On the evening of October 2, Houdon and his three assistants departed Alexandria, Virginia, for the short trip down the Potomac River to Washington's home. They arrived at Mount Vernon's wharf and walked up the steep hill toward the house.

The Washington family was already asleep by the time Houdon knocked on the wooden front door at eleven o'clock. George Washington was expecting them— just not two hours past his bedtime. Houdon and his assistants didn't speak English, and Washington didn't speak French. Fortunately, Washington had hired a French-speaking gentleman from Alexandria to accompany them to Mount Vernon to act as their interpreter.

Houdon brought a letter with him from Paris to deliver to Washington. It was from David Humphreys, one of Washington's aides during the war. Humphreys was happy that Houdon would create a statue of Washington because he understood that people wanted to know what Washington looked like. Humphreys wrote Washington that "not only the present but future generations will be curious to see your figure taken by such an Artist."

> "Not only the present but future generations will be curious to see your figure taken by such an Artist."

Houdon was famous for his ability to sculpt an expression on the faces of his subjects that captured their spirit and personality. And that is exactly what he intended to do for George Washington. While visiting, Houdon observed Washington at Mount Vernon, the home he had improved and expanded over much of his adult life. He could see Washington's ability to blend beauty with function by the graceful arched colonnades that joined the main house to the matching outlying buildings. The road surrounding the grass oval in front of the mansion allowed horse-drawn carriages to drop off people at the front steps, then circle around to the stable. Houdon watched Washington in a wide variety of situations. He saw him supervise the care of the bowling green, the lawn that stretched out like a green blanket in front of the house. Houdon watched as Washington oversaw his slaves plowing a field and as he attended the funeral of a neighbor. The artist observed the way Washington hosted a wedding ceremony at Mount Vernon.

One morning Houdon followed Washington as he met with a man who came to Mount Vernon hoping to sell some horses. Washington looked over the horses and asked the man how much he wanted for them. When he heard the exorbitant price of the horses, a look of indignation crossed his face. Washington thought the man was asking far too much for them. He suggested the horse trader take his horses and leave Mount Vernon. That look was the one Houdon had been waiting for—George Washington was proud, firm, and convinced he was right.

Houdon was ready to get to work. On October 6 and 7, Washington sat for Houdon, who would produce a preliminary bust. The clay he used was likely taken from the ground at Mount Vernon. The artist began adding and removing clay to create the look he wanted, including the wrinkles that creased the forehead of the fifty-three-year-old man. Then he baked the clay bust in the kitchen oven at Mount Vernon. When the bust was finished, Houdon had crafted what he believed was an accurate sculpture of the face and personality of George Washington.

This was just one step toward the final statue, though. Next, Houdon planned to make a life mask of Washington's face. Washington recorded in his diary on October 10, 1785, that he "observed the process for preparing the Plaister of Paris, & mixing of it—according to Mr. Houdon." He described how Houdon made the plaster of Paris he would use. Houdon heated

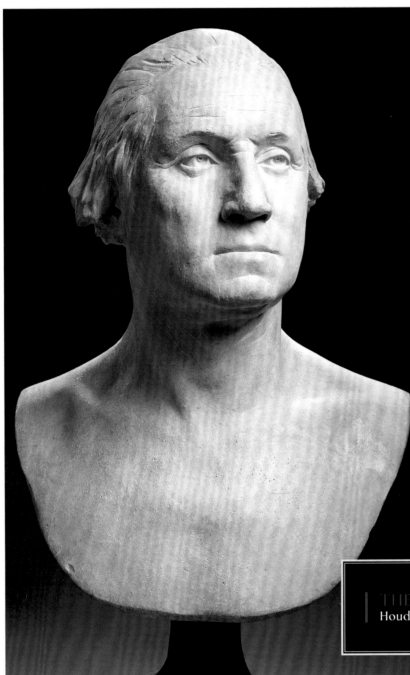

calcium in the oven overnight until hard, pulverized it, and then sifted it. With his plaster ready to make the mask, Houdon gathered his equipment. In the servant's hall, Houdon asked Washington to stretch out on the table—all six feet two inches of him. Washington closed his eyes while Houdon slathered his face with grease so the plaster would not stick to him. Houdon beat water into the dry plaster with a flat iron spoon until it was the consistency of thick cream. After the plaster and water were mixed, Houdon only had four or five minutes before it began to harden, so he worked quickly. He covered Washington's face with plaster and placed quills up his nose so he could breathe while the plaster hardened. Less than ten minutes later, Houdon removed the plaster face cast in one piece.

THE BUST CREATED by Jean-Antoine Houdon in October 1785

From there, Houdon took the face cast and filled it with more plaster. When the plaster in the face cast dried, Houdon removed the life mask from the face cast. He probably had to destroy the face cast as he removed the plaster life mask from it. The result was an exact replica of the face of George Washington that showed every line and fold of skin. To finish the mask, Houdon filled in the nostril holes where the quills had been. He sculpted in Washington's eyes to look open, using the precise measurements he'd taken with calipers as to the size and position of his irises.

Houdon had accomplished everything he intended at Mount Vernon. In addition to making the bust and life mask, he had taken detailed measurements of Washington's body that he would use later to create his statue. The custom of the day was that full-body statues of famous people were made bigger than real life. However, Washington asked Houdon to make his statue life-sized—but not larger than life.

Before he left on October 17, 1785, Houdon gave Washington a gift: the clay bust. Washington placed the bust in his study on a ledge above one of the doors.

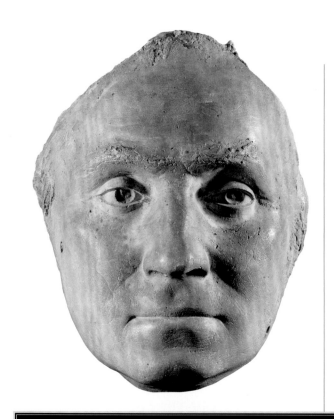

WASHINGTON'S LIFE MASK, made by Jean-Antoine Houdon in 1785 while at Mount Vernon

Houdon returned to his Paris studio with the life mask and his notes of Washington's measurements. For more than two years, the world's best sculptor chipped away at the gleaming white Italian Carrara marble until he created a life-sized statue. On the back of the statue, the artist placed the words "Houdon, French Citizen, 1788";

on the front, "George Washington." The statue was finished before the new Virginia state capitol building was completed, so it was temporality displayed in the Louvre Museum in Paris. On May 14, 1796, Houdon's statue of George Washington was placed in the high-domed rotunda of the Virginia capitol.

CHAPTER THREE

EXAMINING GEORGE WASHINGTON

All three of the pieces of art created by Jean-Antoine Houdon—the life mask, the bust, and the full-body statue—have survived intact for more than 220 years. Unfortunately, Houdon's notes of Washington's exact measurements have not. Houdon's studio in Paris was destroyed during the French Revolution (1789–1799). Schwartz still had his work cut out for him. The Houdon pieces themselves would have to be the starting point for the Mount Vernon project.

•••

When Houdon took measurements to create his George Washington, he had the luxury of being able to touch his model, much like a tailor taking measurements for clothes. Schwartz had no such opportunity. He needed to study the priceless Houdon pieces without damaging—or even touching—them. He knew the perfect technology for the job was available at Arizona State University. He called in Anshuman Razdan, the director of the Partnership for Research in Spatial Modeling (PRISM) and his team of experts. The PRISM laboratory would use a scanner that had the capability to examine three-dimensional (3-D) objects and produce a computerized 3-D scan of them. This would be a perfect way to study each Houdon masterpiece. These scanners have been in use since the 1990s in a wide variety of ways. Toy

JEFFREY SCHWARTZ *(center)* and Anshuman Razdan *(right)* supervise as Scott Van Note *(left)* uses the scanner to take the measurements of the bust of Washington by Houdon at Mount Vernon. The scanner's red laser is the only thing that touches the bust. As the laser bounces off of the bust, the scanner calculates the distance of each point on the bust. All of those measurements together give the precise 3-D measurements of the sculpture.

dinosaurs have been scanned to use as models to create full-size replicas needed for movies, museums, and amusement parks. Clay models of cars are scanned by the auto industry and studied to reduce the number of prototypes required to design a new car style.

Schwartz and the PRISM team traveled to the location of each historical artifact to scan the artifacts. The first stop was Houdon's bust of Washington at Mount Vernon. Houdon's bust was considered to be the best likeness of the man by many who saw it, including Washington's family. Nelly Custis (Eleanor Parke Custis), Washington's step-granddaughter who grew up at Mount Vernon, said years after Washington's death that the bust was "the best representation of Gen. Washington's face" she had ever seen. After Houdon gave Washington the bust in October 1785, it stayed in Washington's study throughout his life and beyond. In 1858 the Mount Vernon Ladies' Association raised the money to buy Mount Vernon. The bust was one of the few original items still in the house. The Houdon bust of Washington is considered to be Mount Vernon's most important artifact.

Schwartz and the PRISM team were aware of the seriousness of their job. They would be scanning an irreplaceable piece of American history. Razdan said, "We were dealing with precious artifacts and could not make a mistake."

They carefully set up the 3-D scanner a safe distance from the bust and scanned it from various angles. The only thing to touch the bust was the scanner's laser beam, similar to a laser pointer. When the beam struck the surface of the bust, it bounced back to the scanner. The scanner then calculated how far that particular point was from the scanner. The scanner measured between one thousand to fifteen hundred specific points per square inch over the entire surface of the bust. A computer then grouped three nearby points together to form triangles. The varying positions and depths of these triangles created a digital image that looked like a mesh. When the scans of the bust were completed, Schwartz and the

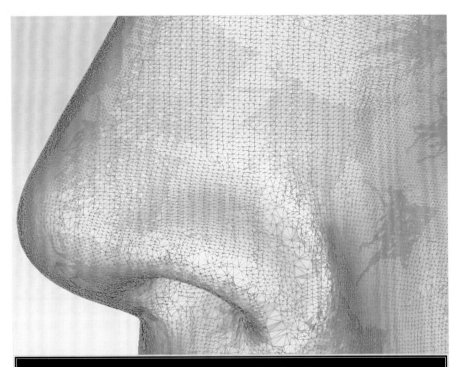

THE 3-D SCANNER converted groups of laser points into triangles, which created a digital "mesh" image.

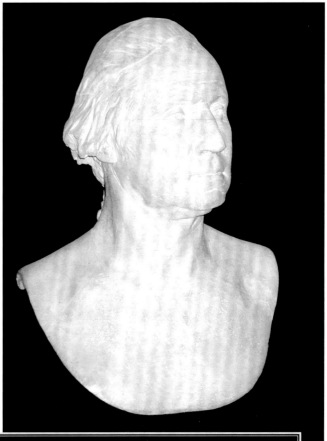

THE 3-D SCAN *(left)* of the Houdon bust is an exact digital copy of the real thing *(right)*.

PRISM team saw a 3-D image that was an exact computer-generated replica of Houdon's bust of George Washington.

Next, they studied Washington's life mask, now owned by the Morgan Library and Museum in New York City. To protect the delicate mask, the Morgan Library keeps it in a locked, climate-controlled vault. The mask was taken out of the vault long enough to allow the team to examine it with the 3-D scanner. They watched as the laser moved over the entire mask, which measures twelve and a half inches from the chin to the top of the head. The result was a 3-D mesh image of every scar, bump, and wrinkle on the face of George Washington on October 10, 1785.

The last of the three Houdon pieces to be scanned was the life-sized statue in Richmond, Virginia. Since it stands on a pedestal, a wooden platform was built around the statue to accommodate the team as they scanned it. For four days, the 3-D scanner worked to produce an exact digital image of the only statue created by a sculptor who had studied Washington in person.

When the PRISM scans of Houdon's bust and mask were compared, Razdan said there was "only one-tenth of a millimeter of difference" between them. The scans were then combined to produce one composite 3-D image. Schwartz and the PRISM team were confident that they had a 3-D digital image of the fifty-three-year-old hero of the American Revolution.

However, George Washington had not always been a hero . . . or fifty-three.

Once upon a time, Washington had been an ambitious young gentleman surveyor in the British colony of Virginia and a loyal subject of Britain's King George. This George Washington, the young Englishman, was one of the three figures Mount Vernon planned to re-create.

CHAPTER FOUR

BECOMING GEORGE WASHINGTON

George Washington was eleven-years-old when his life took an unexpected turn—for the worse. The plan had always been that he would study in Great Britain when he was old enough, like his half brothers before him. Then suddenly his father, Augustine Washington Sr., died and everything changed.

George's mother, Mary Ball Washington, didn't have enough money to send him to a British boarding school. George was disappointed that he would not get to travel or learn a foreign language as he planned. But he did receive an excellent education at home with private tutors until he was about fifteen. To prepare him for running a Virginia plantation,

he studied mathematics, geometry, trigonometry, geography, grammar, conversion of money, land surveying, legal documents, measurements of liquids and solids, cycles of the sun, history, poetry, and speaking.

Augustine Washington's property was divided among his sons when he died, so George became a landowner at a very early age. He inherited Ferry Farm near Fredericksburg on the bank of the Rappahannock River. Young George also inherited ten slaves with the farm.

George was athletic and loved being outdoors, but he also understood that as part of the landowning gentry class of colonial Virginia, he must learn proper manners and social skills. Everything about

Rules of Civility & Decent Behaviour
In Company and Conversation

1 Every Action done in Company, ought to be with Some Sign of Respect, to those that are present.

2 When in Company, put not your Hands to any Part of the Body, not usually Discovered.

3 Shew Nothing to your Friend that may affright him.

4 In the presence of Others Sing not to yourself with a humming Noise, nor Drum with your Fingers or Feet.

5 If you Cough, Sneeze, Sigh, or Yawn, do it not Loud but Privately; and Speak not in your Yawning, but put Your handkerchief or Hand before your face and turn aside.

6 Sleep not when others Speak, Sit not when others stand, Speak not when you Should hold your Peace, walk not on when others Stop.

7 Put not off your Cloths in the presence of Others, nor go out your Chamber half Drest.

8 At Play and at Fire its Good manners to Give Place to the last Commer, and affect not to Speak Louder than ordinary.

9 Spit not in the Fire, nor Stoop low before it neither Put your Hands into the Flames to warm them, nor Set your Feet upon the Fire especially if there be meat before it.

10 When you Sit down, Keep your Feet firm and Even, without putting one on the other or Crossing them.

11 Shift not yourself in the Sight of others nor Gnaw your nails.

12 Shake not the head, Feet, or Legs roul not the Eyes lift not one eyebrow higher than the other wry not the mouth, and bedew no mans face with your Spittle, by approaching too near him when you Speak.

young George must indicate that he was a gentleman, beginning with the way he stood: head up, back arched, shoulders pulled back and down, chest out, and arms gracefully curved at the elbow. He also learned the complicated dance steps that were necessary to attend the frequent balls held in Virginia.

Following his father's death, George grew even closer to Lawrence, his older half brother. Lawrence had inherited the farm called Little Hunting Creek. The modest house consisted of four rooms downstairs and three bedrooms upstairs. Lawrence renamed the property Mount Vernon, in honor of his commander in the British navy, Admiral Edward Vernon.

THIS COPY OF *Rules of Civility & Decent Behaviour in Company and Conversation* was handwritten by George Washington when he was a teenager. It is preserved in the Library of Congress.

George thought it would be a good idea to join the British navy, like Lawrence had done. Together the brothers made all the arrangements, and George even packed his bags. But when his mother found out, she refused to allow young George to go. George was disappointed and began to spend even more of his time at Mount Vernon.

Lawrence Washington was a member of the House of Burgesses, a group of elected representatives in colonial Virginia. He was also the adjutant general and thus in charge of the Virginia militia (a group of local citizens in military service). His wife, Anne, was a member of the wealthy and influential Fairfax family. George became good friends with Anne's brother, George William Fairfax, who was seven years older than he.

The Fairfax family plantation, Belvoir, was located four miles down the Potomac River from Mount Vernon. As a frequent guest at Belvoir, George Washington was exposed to a privileged way of life like he'd never seen before. The mansion was filled with the best things money could buy: beautiful clothing, luxurious furniture, and dishes imported from Europe and Asia.

When George Washington was sixteen, George William Fairfax invited him to accompany him on a working trip into the wilderness to survey the exact size and position of the Fairfax property. Washington jumped at the chance to go. During the trip, George Washington assisted the surveyor with his work. As they traveled, he began a lifelong habit of writing in his journal. He made notes about the weather, the first rattlesnake he saw, and an encounter they had with about thirty Indians who danced a war dance for them. When they stayed overnight at the home of an acquaintance on March 15, 1748, Washington wrote that he "went into the Bed as they call'd it when to my Surprize I found it to be nothing but a Little Straw—Matted together without Sheets or any thing else but only one Thread Bear blanket with double its Weight of Vermin such as Lice Fleas & c. I was glad to get up. . . . I made a Promise not to Sleep so from that time forward chusing rather to sleep in the open Air before a fire."

After the trip was over, Washington decided to become a surveyor himself. This job suited him because it would allow him to use his mathematics skills and be out in the wilderness that he enjoyed. Plus, it was a profession that was considered to be appropriate for a gentleman of his social class. When he was seventeen, he began working as a professional surveyor.

> " . . . best horseman of his age, and the most graceful figure that could be seen on horseback."

With the help of the Fairfax family, he was named as the surveyor of newly established Culpeper County. As he walked through the forests doing his job, Washington admired the beauty of the wilderness land that lay to the west of the colonies. He began buying large tracks of land while in his teens.

By the time he was nineteen, Washington had grown into a tall, handsome young man. Blue-gray eyes complemented the fair skin of his chiseled features. He wore his wavy reddish-brown hair pulled back in a queue—a kind of ponytail—fastened with a black ribbon. Washington worked hard, but he also played hard, keeping busy with billiards, cards, foxhunting, and watching horse races. Like other gentlemen of the day, he trained with a fencing teacher to master the skill of the sword. He broke and trained his own horses—then rode them fast, coaxing them to jump over the highest fences. His skill on a horse was well known. Thomas Jefferson would later describe Washington as the "best horseman of his age, and the most graceful figure that could be seen on horseback."

The same natural athletic grace he displayed while on horseback was also evident in the ballroom. Since George Washington stood much taller than most men, he was easy to spot on the dance floor as he effortlessly guided his dance partners through the intricate steps and patterns of movements required by the minuet, Virginia reel, and cotillion dances. Washington's reputation grew once again— this time as one of the best dancers in all of Virginia.

During this time, George's brother Lawrence developed a serious cough that appeared to be tuberculosis, a serious lung disease. In hopes that Lawrence's health might improve if he traveled to a warmer climate, George accompanied Lawrence to the southern Caribbean Sea.

They arrived in Bridgetown, on the island of Barbados, during an outbreak of smallpox, a highly contagious and often fatal illness at the time. George caught the disease and was seriously ill for nearly a month. Like all survivors, he was left with pitted skin—and immunity from catching the disease again. When George sailed for home on December 22, 1751, he returned with some coral, a delicate fan of coral—and a smallpox scar on his left cheek.

Lawrence didn't fare nearly so well and soon died from tuberculosis. His death left a vacancy in his position as adjutant general of the Virginia militia. George Washington wanted the job, even though he was only twenty years old and had no military experience.

During Lawrence's life, the adjutant general had overseen the military needs of the entire colony. After his death, the leaders of Virginia decided they would divide the colony into three districts, each with its own adjutant general. On December 13, 1752, George Washington was named the adjutant of the smallest of the three districts and given the rank of major. George Washington's military career had begun.

At this time, Britain and France were in a standoff over control of the vast land that lay to the west of the inhabited British colonies. One area of contention was the Ohio River valley (in present-day western Pennsylvania). The British claimed the valley was theirs. The French claimed it was theirs. And the Native American Indians, who had always lived there, wanted to keep it.

Robert Dinwiddie, the governor of Virginia, following orders from King George II, wrote to the commander of the French troops giving him an ultimatum:

leave the area voluntarily or British troops would force them to leave. Dinwiddie wanted his letter delivered as soon as possible, but getting it there would not be easy. Williamsburg, the capital of Virginia, was more than 350 miles from the Ohio River valley where the French were. Much of that distance cut through dangerous Indian land. Plus, it was already late October and winter was coming.

Twenty-one-year-old Major George Washington volunteered to deliver the letter and return with a response. He wanted to prove that he was a valuable leader in the militia. He was perfect for the task. His time as a surveyor had taught him how to survive in the wilderness, yet he was also a British gentleman who could be trusted to properly represent his king.

When Washington left Williamsburg on October 31, 1753, he took with him a few men, including an interpreter for when he met with the French commander. He also hired Christopher Gist, an expert in the frontier and Indian relations.

As Washington's group traveled through the wilderness, winter set in. Most days they were either drenched with cold rain or walking through ankle-deep snow. They finally arrived on November 22 at the fork of the Ohio River (present-day Pittsburgh, Pennsylvania). Washington wrote in his journal that the location was "extremely well suited for a Fort; as it has the absolute Command of both Rivers." (The Monongahela and Allegheny rivers converge here to form the Ohio River.) After leaving the area, they traveled up the Ohio River toward the French encampments.

Washington met the French commander, Jacques Legardeur de Saint-Pierre, and delivered Dinwiddie's ultimatum. On December 15, 1753, the Frenchman responded by writing "as to the summons you send me to retire [leave the area], I do not think myself obliged to obey it." George Washington had the answer he'd come for—stalemate. Britain wanted to control the area, and France wanted to control the area. Both wanted to force the other one out.

The next day, Washington started back toward Williamsburg to deliver the message to Governor Dinwiddie. Travel was difficult in the cold. Washington noted in his journal that the horses were soon weak and "less able to travel every day." On December 26, Washington decided he could travel faster on foot. He changed into his Indian clothing—he likely found these garments more practical for walking in bad weather—and separated from the rest, taking only Christopher Gist with him. Step by step, the two men crunched through the frozen wilderness.

Washington and Gist arrived at the bank of the Allegheny on December 29. Frozen sheets of ice fifty yards wide had formed on each side of the bank, leaving a fast-flowing stream filled with massive chunks of ice in the middle. The only way across the treacherous river was to build a raft. Washington had only one tool: a hatchet.

They went to work. All day the two men cut down trees and lashed them together to make a raft. Finally, at just past sunset, they were ready to launch. Washington climbed aboard the teetering craft carrying his small pack, his gun, and the long pole he planned to use to steer the raft across the river. When both men were balanced and ready, they started across the water.

Huge shards of ice crashed into the raft one after the other. The flimsy raft dipped and rocked. It seemed that any moment they would be overwhelmed and sink. George Washington believed he was going to die.

Looking upriver, Washington saw massive ice floes careening toward them. He had to do something. If only he could stop the raft long enough for the huge pieces to pass them by without hitting them, then maybe they could reach the other side. With every ounce of strength in his body, Washington jammed his navigation pole through the churning water into the muddy river bottom ten feet below the surface. Instantly, water rushed against the pole with such violence that it jerked him off the raft. Washington was swallowed up by the river. He kicked his muscular legs until his head popped up out of the freezing water. He reached for the raft and just barely caught hold of the rough edge. The raft was beaten up by the ice and would not hold together long enough to get to the other side. As Washington drifted downstream in the freezing water, a tiny island in the middle of the river came into view. Letting go of the useless raft, Washington and Gist swam toward the strip of land.

Darkness had fallen by the time they dragged themselves out of the icy water. They were soaked to the skin, and the temperature was falling fast. Washington and Gist shivered through the subfreezing night and hoped they wouldn't freeze to death before morning.

At dawn, they were still alive. Gist suffered from frostbite on all of his fingers and some of his toes. Washington survived without injury. They were relieved to see that during the miserable night, even the middle of the river had frozen solid. Both men walked across the river to the other side and kept going.

Finally, after having been gone for almost two and a half months, Washington arrived in Williamsburg on January 16, 1754. After the more than seven-hundred-mile trip, Washington set out to deliver the letter from the French commander that would determine the next step in the struggle between the rival superpowers of Britain and France. He made his way down the wide, sandy Duke of Gloucester Street. He turned left toward the Governor's Palace. He passed through the elaborate gate into the front courtyard and entered the grand brick house with its tall chimneys and even higher cupola on the top.

Major Washington delivered the letter from the French commander to Governor Dinwiddie and reported to him the arrangements of the French forts and number of troops stationed in them. He also gave Dinwiddie the journal he'd kept of the journey. Dinwiddie was so impressed by Washington and his writings that he ordered the journal published. Major George Washington was moving up in the world.

Since the French troops would not leave territory claimed by the British voluntarily, British troops prepared to remove them by force. Governor Dinwiddie appointed Colonel Joshua Fry to lead the troops of the Virginia regiment of the militia. He named George Washington as his second in command and promoted him to the rank of lieutenant colonel on March 31, 1754.

Dinwiddie ordered them to join the few British who had been sent ahead to begin building a fort at the fork of the Ohio River—the spot Washington had suggested from his previous trip. If anyone obstructed their work, they were to "restrain all such Offenders, and in Case of resistance to make Prisoners of or kill and destroy them." Washington would travel to the area separately from Fry. Twenty-two-year-old Washington left Alexandria, Virginia, on April 2. He had 160 men under

AN EXACT RE-CREATION in Colonial Williamsburg of the Governor's Palace

THE

JOURNAL

OF

MAJOR *George Washington,*

SENT BY THE

Hon. ROBERT DINWIDDIE, Efq;
His Majefty's Lieutenant-Governor, and
Commander in Chief of *Virginia,*

TO THE

COMMANDANT of the *French* Forces

ON

O H I O.

To which are added, the

GOVERNOR's LETTER:

AND A

TRANSLATION of the *French* Officer's Anfwer.

WITH

A New MAP of the Country as far as the
MISSISSIPPI.

WILLIAMSBURGH Printed,
LONDON, Reprinted for *T. Jefferys,* the Corner
of St. *Martin's Lane.*

MDCCLIV.

[Price One Shilling.]

MAJOR GEORGE WASHINGTON'S journal was first published in Virginia in 1754 and then later that year in London. The cover of the Virginia edition shown is one of only eight that have survived.

his command, including his French interpreter, Jacob Van Braam.

Washington arrived to find French troops hiding in a nearby ravine—an apparent ambush. As the commanding officer, he made the decision to attack them. It was the first time Washington had been in battle. When the smoke cleared after the fifteen-minute skirmish, one of Washington's men had been killed. Ten French soldiers and their leader, Joseph Coulon de Villiers de Jumonville, were dead, and twenty-one were taken as prisoners. One man escaped and ran to Fort Duquesne with the news of the attack.

Washington described the battle in a letter to his brother John Augustine Washington: "I fortunately escaped without a wound, tho' the right Wing where I stood was exposed to & received all the Enemy's fire and was the part where the man was killed & the rest wounded. I can with truth assure you, I heard Bulletts whistle and believe me there was something charming in the sound."

Immediately after the battle, Washington knew he had a problem. Jacob Van Braam explained that the French prisoners claimed they were on a peaceful mission and that they had a letter to give to any British people they encountered. The letter claimed the land belonged to France and that the British had to leave the area or be forced out. The message was similar to the one Washington delivered to the French just a few months before.

Washington did not believe that de Jumonville and his men had been on a peaceful mission. But Washington was convinced of two things. First, because the French did not seek him out to deliver a message, they must have been spying on the movements of his troops. Second, he believed that the French would retaliate.

At their camp at Great Meadows, Washington and his men prepared for an attack. They built a fort out of white oak trees buried upright in the ground. The circular palisade defense was fifty-three feet across, with a deep battle trench around it. They called it Fort Necessity and flew the British flag over it.

While waiting for the French to come, Washington got a message that the hoped-for reinforcements from his commanding officer would not arrive—and that he had been promoted to colonel.

Gunfire split the air of Fort Necessity at nine in the morning on July 3, 1754. The French commander of the attack was Louis Coulon de Villiers, the half brother of the slain de Jumonville. Colonel Washington's four hundred men were

AN ACCURATE RE-CREATION of Fort Necessity as it looked in 1754. Later in life, Washington bought the land where he and his troops had built the fort.

33

outnumbered by at least three to one. At eight that evening, Washington knew it was hopeless and agreed to discuss terms of surrender. He sent Jacob Van Braam to hear what the French had to say. At about midnight, after some negotiations, a surrender document written in French was prepared and Washington signed it.

Soon after, Colonel Washington found out what the French document actually said. The document Washington signed stated that he agreed that Fort Necessity was built on French land and that de Jumonville had been *assassinated*. Washington claimed he had been deceived by Van Braam over the word "assassinated" and later wrote, "whatever his motives were for so doing, certain it is, he called it the *death*, or the *loss*, of the Sieur [literally, "sir"] Jumonvillle. So we received and so we understood it, until, to our great surprise and mortification, we found it otherwise in a literal translation."

Suddenly Washington's name was known on both sides of the Atlantic Ocean. In Virginia he was considered a hero. In Great Britain, he was considered a courageous colonial who lacked experience. In France he was considered a villain who had assassinated de Jumonville. The actions of George Washington on the day de Jumonville was killed had a far-reaching effect. The skirmish marked the beginning of the French and Indian War (1754–1763).

To command the war, Great Britain sent one of its most experienced leaders, Major General Edward Braddock. He arrived with twenty-four hundred British soldiers. Braddock also took charge of the colonial militia troops, but because they were not professional soldiers, he expected little of them. However, the reputation of one colonial had impressed him: George Washington.

In early March 1755, General Braddock invited Washington to join the family of officers and aides-de-camp who surrounded him. From Braddock, Washington learned how to supply and lead an army. Braddock was also an expert in the European style of warfare, where men armed with guns and bayonets lined up shoulder to shoulder and met their enemy on an open battlefield. But Washington knew a few things Braddock did not know—like how to fight in the American wilderness. Washington suggested to Braddock that European war tactics would not work in America—that the soldiers needed to learn to fight like the Indians who used trees for cover. Braddock ignored the young colonial.

Braddock's first goal was to attack Fort Duquesne. The French had taken over this prime location at the fork of the Ohio. The British wanted it for themselves. Braddock and his men pushed toward their target using the same road forged by Washington the year before. As they went, they enlarged the small road to about twelve feet wide to accommodate their large wagons and cannons. Since many trees had to be cleared away, progress was slow—so slow that Braddock decided to divide his troops. He took half of his men and pushed ahead. The other half made their way slowly as they built the road.

Washington was to have been with Braddock, but on June 14, 1754, he fell ill and was unable to travel. He was determined to be present for the attack on Fort Duquesne, though, and made Braddock promise to send for him when the men neared the fort. Washington took almost three weeks to recover, but Braddock was true to his word and sent for Washington when the troops got within seven miles of the fort. On July 8, Washington arrived in a covered wagon to rejoin Braddock. The next day, the best horseman in Virginia pulled himself up on a horse for the first time since he became sick three and a half weeks before. To tolerate sitting in a saddle after his long bout with dysentery (severe diarrhea), he put cushions under his bottom.

> "...unusual Hallooing and whooping of the enemy"

He joined Braddock's thirteen hundred men as they crossed the Monongahela River and rode into the thick forest toward Fort Duquesne. About ten o'clock that morning, Washington heard an "unusual Hallooing and whooping of the enemy."

Braddock's men were under attack by three hundred French soldiers and Indian warriors who stayed hidden under the cover of the trees. The British regulars were filled with terror and confusion when they realized their fellow soldiers were being shot down one by one by an enemy they couldn't even see. Some British soldiers ran away, while the Virginia militiamen took cover and began to fight.

All thoughts of his weakened condition vanished as Washington fought the French and Indians. His horse was shot, so he jumped up on another one. Bullets flew so close to his head that two of them left holes in his hat. His second horse was shot down under him. He jumped up on a third and kept fighting.

Everything was chaotic in the haze of musket smoke. Then Washington saw that Braddock was wounded—and that he was the only aide still standing. He immediately went to his commanding officer. While under constant fire, Washington loaded the bleeding general into a small covered cart. Washington gathered some troops to cover them as he took Braddock back across the Monongahela and away from the fighting.

After Washington got the general a safe distance from the battle, Braddock ordered him to get the other half of his men—the ones who had been cutting the road behind them—to come to him with supplies for the wounded, retreating soldiers.

Washington jumped up on his horse and galloped off to carry out Braddock's orders. Despite his weak condition, he had a job to do. The second division of men was forty miles away. Washington stayed in the saddle as the sun set. He stayed in the saddle as darkness covered the road and the surrounding forest. And he stayed in the saddle as the sun rose in the east.

Sometime the next morning, George Washington finally met up with the other half of the troops. He had ridden throughout the night to complete his mission.

When the second division caught up with Braddock's group, the scene shocked Washington. He would never forget the groaning and crying as men lay dying.

A REMNANT OF THE BRADDOCK ROAD. Washington had General Braddock buried in the middle of the road, not far from this spot. In 1804, Braddock's remains were moved to a nearby hill. Today his grave, marked by a large monument, is part of the Fort Necessity National Battlefield in southwestern Pennsylvania about sixty miles from Pittsburgh.

Of the thirteen hundred men who were involved in the battle, over eight hundred men were killed or wounded. What was left of Braddock's troops retreated and camped about one mile from Great Meadows, the former site of Fort Necessity.

General Braddock died from his injuries three days after the battle. Washington said a few words over his body and had him buried in the middle of the road they had built. Braddock's army marched over his grave so that the enemy would not be able to find it—and possibly desecrate his remains.

When the news of Braddock's defeat reached Virginia, rumors circulated that

George Washington had been killed. When he was finally strong enough to write to his brother John Augustine on July 18, he revealed both his dry sense of humor and his modesty by saying,

> As I have heard since my arrival at this place, a circumstantial account of my death and dying Speech, I take this early opportunity of contradicting the first, and of assuring you that I have not, as yet, composed the latter. But by the all powerful dispensations of Providence, I have been protected beyond all human probability & expectation for I had 4 Bullets through my Coat, and two Horses shot under me yet although death was leveling my companions on every side of me escaped unhurt.

When Washington wrote to his brother in July 1755, he had no way to know that in just over twenty years he would share a battlefield with British soldiers again, . . . but then they would be his enemy.

CHAPTER FIVE

WASHINGTON AT NINETEEN

A year or so after General Braddock was defeated in battle, a British soldier died at Fort William Henry in New York and George Washington lost his first tooth. These two events would intersect more than 250 years later.

MAKING FACES

From the PRISM scans of Houdon's bust, life mask, and statue, Schwartz knew how George Washington looked at the age of fifty-three. But the goal of the Mount Vernon project was to depict Washington as he appeared at the ages of nineteen, forty-five, and fifty-seven. To accomplish this, Schwartz would use the information gained from the Houdon pieces as a foundation and build on it.

The first step was to find out more about Washington's jawbones. The way a person's face looks on the outside is influenced by the size and shape of the jawbones as well as the teeth. The key to finding the answers about George Washington's jawbones was that he was missing his teeth. Although Washington took good care of his teeth, gum disease, possibly caused by eighteenth-century medications laced with mercury, caused him to lose one tooth after another throughout his adult life. Finally, he was missing so many teeth he had to wear dentures.

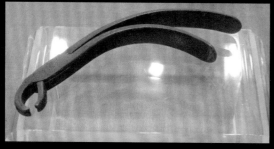

ACCORDING TO SOME ACCOUNTS, these forceps were made by a blacksmith near Somerset, New Jersey, and were used to pull one of Washington's teeth during the American Revolution.

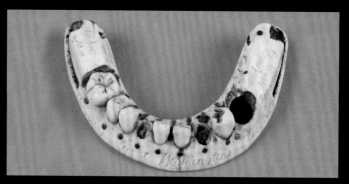

JOHN GREENWOOD MADE THIS LOWER DENTURE for Washington in 1789. Human teeth are attached to the base, which is carved from hippopotamus ivory. Greenwood made a hole in the base to accommodate Washington's remaining tooth. The following is engraved into the ivory: "Under jaw. This is Great Washington's teeth by J. Greenwood. First one made by J. Greenwood, Year 1789."

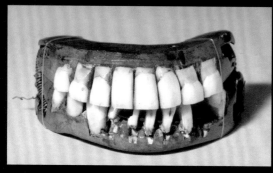

CONTRARY TO THE MYTH, none of Washington's dentures were made of wood. This set from the collection at Mount Vernon has a lead base. It is held together with heavy springs intended to help the dentures stay in his mouth. The upper plate contains cow and horse teeth; and the lower, human teeth.

JOHN GREENWOOD MADE THIS SET of dentures for Washington sometime before 1798. The bottom half is carved from hippopotamus ivory. On the top, ivory teeth were attached to a gold alloy palate.

Washington's dentures, the same ones that caused him so much pain, misery, and embarrassment, have been preserved today. Schwartz and the PRISM team scanned Washington's dentures from the collections at Mount Vernon, the Samuel D. Harris National Museum of Dentistry, and the New York Academy of Medicine.

The PRISM scans of these dentures revealed the shape of Washington's jaws. With this information, Schwartz could create a digital image of Washington's jawbones by combining a scan of his denture with a scan of another man's bones. He wanted to use the jawbones of someone who was similar in size to Washington, so he measured the jaw area of the Houdon bust at Mount Vernon. By chance, Brenda Baker, an anthropologist at Arizona State University, had access to a collection of historic remains that included the jawbone of a man about Washington's size. The bone came from a British soldier who was probably about twenty years old when he died during the French and Indian War. Although it wasn't necessary to use the bones of this long-dead soldier—whose name is lost to history—it seemed

WHEN GEORGE WASHINGTON'S LAST TOOTH was pulled, John Greenwood kept it as a souvenir. He preserved the tooth in a small gold container with a glass top and carried it around with him. The tooth can be seen through the glass of the oval container on the bottom right. Engraved on the side of the gold case: "In New York 1790 Jn Greenwood made Pres Geo Washington a whole set of teeth. The enclosed tooth is the last one which grew in his head."

appropriate. This unknown man and George Washington were about the same size and age, and both had fought in the same war.

Schwartz and the PRISM team scanned the mandible—the lower jawbone—of the British soldier with the 3-D scanner. Then to see if the jawbone would fit in Washington's body, he layered the image of the jawbone over the image of the Houdon bust. The fit was not perfect—the mandible from the soldier was smaller than Washington's had been.

Schwartz realized he needed to be able to manipulate the computer images in ways that had never been done before. When he explained to the PRISM team what he needed, they wrote cutting-edge software to give him the flexibility he required. This software would give Schwartz the ability to adjust the computer image of the soldier's bone to duplicate the size and shape of Washington's bones. This would be done in two stages.

The first stage would adjust the size of the mandible. To do this, the digital image of the soldier's mandible was once again layered over the digital image of Washington's bust. Using the new software, Schwartz "added" some bone to the image of the soldier's jaw until it was a perfect anatomical fit within the bust of Washington's head.

The second stage would adjust the shape of the mandible. To do this, the image of Washington's denture from the New York Academy of Medicine (the shape of the denture would have exactly followed Washington's jawbones) was layered over the scan of the

DIGITAL "BONE" (in yellow) was added to the soldier's mandible (in blue) until it fit properly within the Washington bust.

newly resized British soldier's jawbone. Layering these images showed them that the shape of the soldier's jawbone was wider than Washington's. Using the new software, Schwartz adjusted the angle of the soldier's mandible so that it exactly matched the angle of Washington's denture.

To re-create Washington's maxilla (upper jaw), this same technique was used by adjusting the soldier's maxilla to mirror the size and shape of the copy of Washington's upper denture from the Smithsonian Museum of American History.

When this phase was complete, Schwartz and the PRISM team had digital scans that were the exact shape and size of George Washington's upper and lower jawbones—when he was fifty-three years old. To ensure accuracy, Schwartz and the PRISM team layered the digital image of Washington's jaws over the Houdon bust and found they were a perfect anatomical fit. With accurate images of Washington's jaws, Schwartz could make necessary changes to the images that would reflect Washington's jawbones at different times in his life.

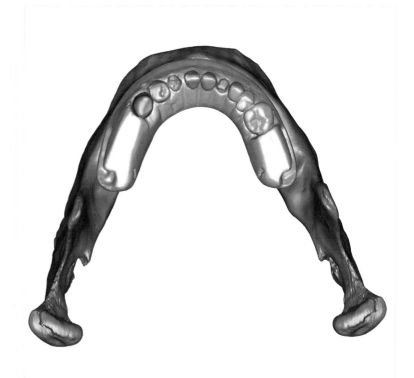

THE IMAGE OF WASHINGTON'S DENTURE (in white and gray) is layered over the British soldier's mandible (in blue). The PRISM software allowed the team to adjust the bone to fit the shape of Washington's jaw.

First, they would take the image of Washington at fifty-three and age him four years to depict him during his presidential inauguration. After a tooth is pulled, the jawbone where the tooth had been slowly begins to wear away. Washington's denture proves that he had only one tooth remaining in his mouth when he was fifty-seven. Because Washington experienced massive tooth loss, he would also have had massive bone loss in his jaws.

To reflect this change, Schwartz used his knowledge as an anthropologist to digitally remove bone from the image of Washington's jawbones. The result was that the digital images of the upper and lower jawbones of George Washington were aged. They looked as they would have when he was inaugurated at the age of fifty-seven.

Next, Schwartz took this new image and layered it over the Houdon bust. The bone loss caused a change in the size and shape of Washington's jaw. Therefore, the facial features had to be adjusted to fit the bones beneath them. The result was that Washington's face looked shorter than before.

Schwartz gave him a bit more fullness in his face to accurately reflect changes that naturally occur as people age. At last, Schwartz and the PRISM team looked into the computer-generated face of fifty-seven-year-old President George Washington.

With an accurate image of Washington at fifty-seven, Schwartz could de-age him

twelve years to reflect how he looked when he was commander in chief of the Continental Army. To make him younger, Schwartz added some bone mass back to Washington's jaws to reflect how they would have looked when he was forty-five years old. Next, he layered the jaw images over the image of Washington at fifty-seven. From there, Schwartz adjusted the outside facial features to match the bones below. Schwartz tightened up the skin on Washington's face to make the image look younger. With these finishing touches, they saw the face of General Washington.

•••

The final step was to take the image of forty-five-year-old Washington and de-age him to nineteen. Washington still had all of his teeth when he was in his teens. Therefore, to create an accurate image of his facial bones at this time in his life, Schwartz added still more bone mass and a full set of teeth to Washington's jaws. He layered the images of the jaws of Washington at nineteen over the image of Washington at the age of forty-five. Then he adjusted the facial features to fit the bones beneath. Of all the adjustments, this one made the biggest difference because it changed the shape of his face. To illustrate why this made such a difference, consider a hamburger: if the meat patty is thick, the bun halves are farther apart, but if the meat patty is thin, the bun halves are closer together. When Washington's teeth filled his mouth, his jawbones were positioned farther apart. The result was that at nineteen, Washington's face looked longer and thinner than it did later in life.

Schwartz removed all traces of sagging skin and added some fat into his cheeks that would normally be present in a nineteen-year-old. Knowing that the cartilage continues to grow throughout the years, Schwartz slightly shortened the teenager's nose and earlobes. At last, they looked into the virtual face of George Washington as a teenager. The image of nineteen-year-old Washington's head was finished, but he still needed a body.

MEASUREMENTS FROM THE NECK DOWN

To investigate the shape of Washington's body when he was a teenager, Schwartz

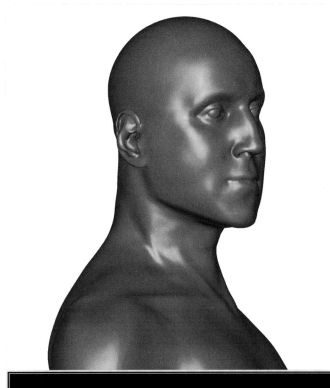

THE COMPUTER-GENERATED 3-D image of Washington at the age of nineteen

considered many different factors. Washington described himself in letters to his tailor in London. He said he was "6 feet high and proportionally made – if anything rather slender than thick for a person of that highth with pretty long arms and thighs." Captain George Mercer, Washington's aide-de-camp at Fort Necessity and the Braddock campaign, said Washington measured "six feet two inches in his stockings . . . with well-developed muscles, indicating great strength. . . . His bones and joints are large, as are his feet and hands." Mercer also called Washington "wide shouldered" and said he had "a clear though rather colorless pale skin, which burns with the sun." And of course, Schwartz knew his history. Washington had been a surveyor—a strenuous, physical job—as well as an outdoorsman and a horseman. The man who would become the face on the dollar bill had a body well suited for hard, physical work.

Although no clothing worn by Washington during this time in his life survives, additional information came from Linda Baumgarten, curator of textiles and costumes at Colonial Williamsburg, a historic site in Virginia. Baumgarten used her knowledge and expertise to bring the team a better understanding of the shape of George Washington's body. Eighteenth-century, upper-class families like the Washingtons clothed both girls and boys in stays. This was a corset filled with thin pieces of wood or baleen whalebone worn around the chest. Baumgarten explained, "Stays molded the body from an early age and helped teach genteel posture and movement. As a result, men and women learned how to stand with dropped shoulders, prominent chest, and erect posture." George Washington would have worn stays when he was a very young child. This would have shaped his body into the proper posture for a gentleman. This is why men depicted in eighteenth-century portraits seem to have a different body shape than modern men.

Schwartz combined this information with his understanding about how a man matures to determine the shape of Washington's body when he was nineteen years old. He stood at his full height, was thin and muscular, and weighed about 175 pounds.

CREATING THE ROUGH REPRESENTATIONS

After two and a half years of work, Schwartz and the PRISM team had produced accurate 3-D computer images of the heads and bodies of George Washington at nineteen, forty-five, and fifty-seven years of age. The next step was to turn them into something physical.

The computer files of the 3-D images of Washington were sent to Kreysler and Associates, a custom fabrication company in American Canyon, California. Kreysler specializes in all kinds of construction with composite materials, and the company has worked on a wide variety of projects, such as building film sets for movies, re-creating missing elements in historic buildings, and taking a small plastic toy and creating a forty-foot-tall copy, as in the blue bear at the Colorado Convention Center.

Kreysler's role was to take the data from the computer files and use the data to create physical representations of Washington. Each head and body began as a block of plastic foam and was cut into shape by the computerized mill. In just a few minutes, the images of Washington that had previously existed only on a computer screen became reality that could be touched. The three rigid, plastic foam heads were recognizable as George Washington. Kreysler and Associates then shipped the three heads and the three bodies of George Washington from their mill in California to StudioEIS in New York City.

A COMPUTER-CONTROLLED MILLING MACHINE turns a digital representation of Washington's head into a physical one by cutting away material from a block of foam until only the head remains.

StudioEIS, founded by Ivan and Elliot Schwartz (no relation to Jeffrey H. Schwartz), is a team of artists that creates 3-D portraits that bring to life the character and personality of its subjects. Studio EIS's work is featured at the National Constitution Center, the Gettysburg National Military Park, the National Infantry Museum, the National Museum of the Marine Corps, the

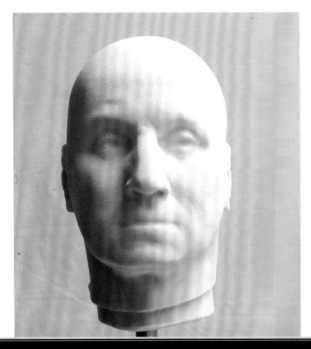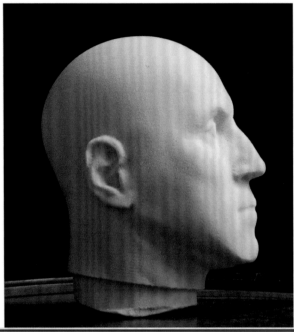

FINISHED FOAM HEADS. On the left is Washington at the age of fifty-seven. On the right is Washington at forty-five.

Smithsonian National Museum of Natural History, the New York Yankees Museum, the NCAA Hall of Champions, and many other places.

Long before the foam heads arrived, Ivan Schwartz collaborated on creative decisions with Jeffrey Schwartz and Mount Vernon's James Rees and Ann Bay. They discussed many details about how each of the three re-creations should look, including the facial expressions and the body positions. The process fascinated Ivan Schwartz, who said, "Part of the fun of this project was that

the research into what Washington looked like was continuing, so the whole circle was not closed—there were still questions to be resolved."

StudioEIS took heads through several different phases before they were completed. The Kreysler foam head gave StudioEIS the shape of Washington's head and face, but plastic foam wasn't the ideal medium for re-creating lifelike details. For that, they needed copies made of clay. The first step in making clay heads was to make a plastic mold of each foam head that came from the Kreysler mill. Next, the plastic molds were packed with water-based sculptor's clay. When the molds were removed, they revealed the three clay heads of George Washington. The smooth, clay heads still didn't look like a real person because they lacked details such as natural folds of skin, wrinkles, and facial expressions. Since the heads were clay, though, these lifelike details could soon be added by the sculptor.

To breathe life into the clay faces, StudioEIS brought in British artist and master sculptor Stuart Williamson. Williamson's goal was to take each expressionless clay head of George Washington and "imbue him with a sense of life and the moment."

Williamson gathered as much information as possible to prepare to create the portrait sculptures. He studied the life of George Washington, portraits of him painted by various artists, Houdon's bust, and the forensic evidence uncovered by Schwartz.

The exhibit at Mount Vernon would portray nineteen-year-old Washington, before his trip to Barbados. The exhibit would depict him working as a surveyor who had stopped to look over the land ahead and make a note in his book. Once Williamson had a clear idea of the

SCULPTOR STUART WILLIAMSON looks at the clay copies of the foam heads (shown in gray) before beginning his work. His goal is to give each Washington head "a sense of life and the moment."

49

expression that should be on the face of young Washington, he was ready to begin.

Usually, Williamson creates his portrait sculptures "from inside out." He starts with a foundation, then adds soft clay as he considers how the underlying bone and muscle affects the way people look. But this project was different. This time, he would begin his work with the smooth clay heads.

Williamson cut into the clay to establish for himself the underlying bone structure. His understanding of the anatomy beneath the skin allowed him to accurately sculpt the surface of the skin. Williamson modeled the clay to give Washington's face a confident, optimistic expression as he gazed "off into the distance as if surveying." As he worked, Williamson kept in mind where Washington's eyes would be focused. Knowing that every movement of the eyeball changes the shape of the eyelid, he sculpted the eyes and eyelids to reflect an anatomically correct position.

Williamson's clay sculptures were lifelike, but they were still not the last step. When Williamson finished sculpting the clay head of nineteen-year-old George Washington, a reusable plastic mold was made of it. Next, the plastic mold was filled with melted, flesh-colored wax, made from beeswax mixed with synthetic wax. The goal was to leave the wax in the mold long enough to allow the outside to harden while the middle was still liquid. After about an hour, the liquid middle was poured out. This left the middle hollow and the sides with a layer of wax about a half inch thick. The creamy yellow wax head was then released from the mold, to reveal a wax replica of Williamson's sculpture. This wax head was the final head, the one that would go in the exhibit. The process of making a piece mold and then a wax head was the same for the other two Washington heads.

To create Washington's hands, StudioEIS found a model whose hands fit the size and age of young Washington. The model held his hands in the desired position—his right hand as if he was holding a writing instrument and his left as if holding a notebook—while the mold was made. When they were finished, the molds were filled with Elvex, a plastic and wax mixture. Elvex was used on the hands because it is more resistant to touching and possible damage.

Next, StudioEIS brought in two more experts. One was Sue Day, an artist from Great Britain. She would paint the wax heads, the hands, and work on the hair. The second was Steven Horak, a master wigmaker who creates museum-quality hairpieces.

To depict George Washington accurately, the team had to get his coloring right. Ivan Schwartz, Stuart Williamson, Sue Day, and Steven Horak collaborated to determine the appropriate skin tone, hair color, and eye color. The team consulted portraits of Washington and historical descriptions of him. Another factor that influenced their color choices was that George Washington's family had originally come from England. Washington had the common coloring of many people with English ancestry—fair skin, reddish-brown hair, and blue eyes. Since both Williamson and Day are British, they were very familiar with people who have this coloring. They also understand how fair skin, like Washington's, is affected by the wind and the sun and even how tiredness affects the paleness of the skin. Not only did Day and Williamson understand the colors needed for the wax heads, they were experts in the wax-figure medium since both had previously worked at Madame Tussauds Wax Museum in London.

Washington's eyes were often described as being blue gray in color. The artists looked at a collection of acrylic eyeballs in various shades of blue and chose the one set that best matched that description and blended well with Washington's fair complexion.

To set the realistic-looking acrylic eyeballs into place, Williamson would first need to remove the wax eyeballs from the head. Williamson used tools he'd developed through the years for this delicate process. He lit a small lamp and held a metal stick over the flame to get it hot. Then he pressed the hot tool into the center of the wax eyeball to melt a small hole in the wax. His next tool consisted of a metal rod with a round ball about an inch across on the end. He heated the ball over the lamp's flame and then reached through the hollow neck of the wax head to press the hot ball into the wax behind the wax eyes. Through the first hole he made, he could see the wax liquefy. As the smell of melted wax filled the air, he watched carefully until

the eyelid was thin enough to look like a real eyelid—about an eighth of an inch. He took the blue-gray eyes with clear whites and placed them inside the wax head. Williamson took care to make sure the eyes were positioned correctly so they looked as if they were focused on a specific point in the distance.

Sue Day took over the work at this point. Day covered the entire wax head with a base coat of fleshy-pink-colored oil-based paint. When it was dry, Day prepared her painter's palette by squirting out fifteen different shades of paint. These were the colors needed to paint Washington's face. Day applied thin layers of paint, slowly building a natural-looking depth of color, to create the look of real skin. With great skill, Day painted his fair skin and ruddy cheeks. Day added realistic details such as a slight five o'clock shadow, as if that moment in time occurred at the end of a long workday when his beard was starting to show. To accomplish this look, she used thin paint on a brush and randomly splattered it on his face. The effect looks so real that if you could touch his cheek, you'd expect to feel his whiskers beginning to grow.

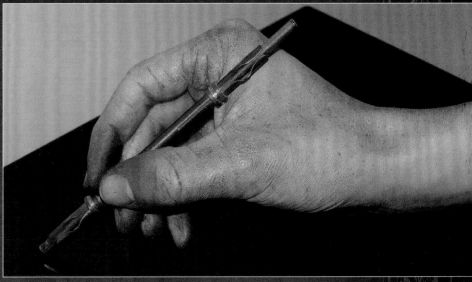

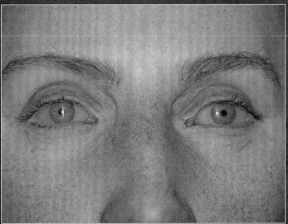

YOUNG WASHINGTON'S HANDS *(above)* were painted with realistic details including the appearance of graphite from his writing instrument that would have rubbed off on his fingers.

ARTIST SUE DAY *(top)* works on young Washington's hairline to get the right shape.

SUE DAY PLACED each eyebrow and eyelash hair one by one in Washington's face *(above)*.

WIGMAKER STEVEN HORAK *(left)* curls young Washington's hair using a tool similar to those used in the eighteenth century.

She used the same expertise and attention to detail to paint the teenager's hands. She added crescents of white at the base of his fingernails and the natural coloring in the creases of his skin. With extraordinary realism, Day painted the fingertips of his right hand to look as if the writing instrument had left graphite dust on his hands.

The hair came next. Many genuine samples of George Washington's hair exist because preserving locks of hair was common in the eighteenth century. The team of artists studied a sample of Washington's hair from the collections at Mount Vernon. His hair was reddish brown and had a slight wavy texture. From a hair merchant in London, the artists ordered a perfect match for his hair. The cost of the hair for nineteen-year-old Washington was about three hundred dollars.

Day and Horak worked together on Washington's hair. Each one worked on a different aspect of the job. Horak made custom wigs to cover the back of the head. Day inserted hair directly into the wax at the front, the sides, and the bottom of the back of the head. To do this, Day uses a tool that looks like a needle with the eye cut in half. She catches the end of a single hair with her tool and pushes it directly into the wax. She positions each hair to make it look as if it is growing naturally out of the wax head. According to Day, one of the most crucial decisions is creating the correct hairline because it "is important to get right because it shapes Washington's face." Over five days, one human hair at a time, Day inserted thousands of strands per square inch using smooth, quick, and precise movements.

Horak and Day decided where the inserted hair would stop and the wig would start. To begin his part of the hair, Horak measured the back of the wax head to see what size the finished wig should be. Next, he made the base of the wig out of netting. Horak used a tool similar to a crochet hook to attach hair to the net wig base—one strand at a time.

Day wasn't yet finished, though. Next, she inserted young Washington's facial hair one strand at a time. This time she used tightly curled human hair as she blended the spot where the hair on his temple stopped and his sideburns began. For his eyebrows, Day used hair in four different shades—lighter, darker, redder, and browner—to create a realistic look. She even added some random, stray hairs that always grow above the eyebrows on the faces of real people. She aligned and trimmed each hair, taking care to shape his eyebrows to match portraits of Washington.

With every strand in its proper place, Day and Horak discussed young Washington's hairstyle. Horak curled his long hair to give it a natural-looking wave and then smoothed it back in a queue, a fashionable style of the time period. It was secured with a plain black ribbon, just as Washington would have done more than 250 years ago.

The head and hands of nineteen-year-old Washington were complete.

CLOTHING FOR THE MAN

The young gentleman still needed to be properly dressed. StudioEIS called in Henry Cooke, a tailor who is a leading expert in creating accurate reproductions of historic clothing. Washington himself was an enormous help in determining the style of clothing, having written specific instructions as to how he wanted his clothing to look. Cooke also studied a painting from the National Gallery in London titled *Mr. and Mrs. Andrews* by Thomas Gainsborough. This piece of art from around 1750

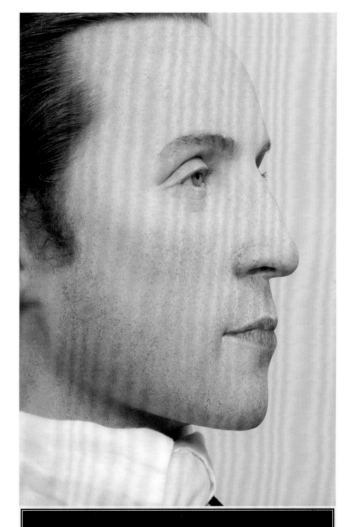

THE FACE OF nineteen-year-old Washington. The artists who worked on the project made sure to capture the facial color and texture of a young man accustomed to working outdoors in the sun.

shows the way a young British gentleman dressed while hunting.

Working in collaboration with James Rees and Ann Bay from Mount Vernon, Cooke combined this historic information with his knowledge of eighteenth-century clothing to design the appropriate garments for Washington as a surveyor. Cooke made plush breeches out of woolen nap, thicker than velvet, which would have kept Washington warm while in the wilderness. Leggings covered his lower legs from his knees to his shoes.

Neal Hurst, a tailor who specializes in crafting eighteenth-century clothing, made his linen shirt. During this period, men didn't wear underwear, so their shirts were generally down to their knees and had long sleeves. For historical accuracy, Hurst made this a "work" shirt from a lower-quality linen and without a ruffle down the front or at the sleeves. Hurst also made the stock, a wide strip of fabric worn around the neck.

Another craftsman, Ken Treese, studied the construction techniques of sturdy work shoes from Washington's time that were found in Maryland. Treese felt these shoes would have been a good choice for a surveyor of the Virginia wilderness. He re-created them using the same sorts of tools and techniques used during the 1700s. The handmade shoes took Treese more than twelve hours to make.

Finally, all the pieces were finished. For the first time in over two centuries, it was possible to see George Washington as he would have looked when he was nineteen years old. He was a rugged young man who was as comfortable in a ballroom as he was in the backwoods. Working as a surveyor, he lived off the land and saw the endless potential and great beauty of the unspoiled wilderness of America.

Both the man and the land had within them the possibility of greatness.

GEORGE WASHINGTON as he would have looked at the age of nineteen

CHAPTER SIX

BECOMING GENERAL WASHINGTON

May 4, 1775, was a good day for traveling—warm and clear. Forty-three-year-old George Washington said good-bye to his wife, Martha, and turned his horse toward the gate of Mount Vernon. He made his way north toward Philadelphia to attend the Second Continental Congress as a delegate from Virginia.

The Congress convened at the Pennsylvania State House (now known as Independence Hall) on May 10 to discuss the deteriorating relationship between King George III and his British colonies. The bond seemed to be beyond repair, since His Majesty's troops had recently killed ninety-five colonists at battles in Lexington and Concord in Massachusetts. The time had come for every colonial citizen to choose a side. They would either stay loyal to King George and his troops or they would support the American patriots. The latter choice would likely mean war and rebellion.

George Washington knew which side he was on. In a letter dated May 31, 1775, to his dear friend George William Fairfax, Washington explained about what had happened at Lexington and Concord. He ended by saying, "Unhappy it is though to reflect, that a Brother's Sword has been sheathed in a Brother's breast, and that, the once happy and peaceful plains of America are either to be drenched

THE FIRST PORTRAIT painted of Washington. In 1772, Charles Willson Peale painted him wearing the Virginia militia uniform that he'd worn during the French and Indian War—possibly the same uniform he took with him to Philadelphia three years later.

As his fellow delegates discussed the situation, George Washington said little. However, since he wore his old war uniform to Congress every day, they likely knew how he felt. George Washington, a man who had personally experienced the horrors of war, was willing to fight for independence from Great Britain.

Finally, the Congress agreed they must defend themselves against the aggression of the British troops. But that would require an army, and an army would require a commander. On June 15, 1775, John Adams nominated George Washington to command the army, and Samuel Adams seconded the motion. Washington was admired and respected by every man in attendance, and he was the only delegate with any military experience. He was unanimously elected to become the commander in chief of the Continental Army, an army that didn't exist yet. John Adams wrote his wife, Abigail, that Congress had chosen, the "modest and virtuous, the amiable, generous and brave George Washington Esqr., to be the General of the American Army."

On June 18, 1775, George Washington wrote Martha to explain that Congress

with Blood, or Inhabited by Slaves. Sad alternative! But can a virtuous Man hesitate in his choice?"

had asked him to lead the defense of the "American Cause" and that he must accept the position. He tenderly explained to her that he would "feel no pain from the Toil, or the danger of the Campaign—My unhappiness will flow, from the uneasiness I know you will feel at being left alone."

General George Washington, commander in chief of the Continental Army, arrived at his headquarters in Cambridge, Massachusetts, and took control of the army the next day, July 3, 1775. The men had no military training. Washington would need to teach them the basics—everything from having proper respect for their commanding officers to how to guard the camp and to where to build the latrines.

When James Thacher, an army surgeon, saw the commander in chief for the first time on July 20, 1775, he wrote in his journal,

> I have been much gratified this day with a view of General Washington. His excellency was on horseback, in company with several military gentlemen. It was not difficult to distinguish him from all the others;

his personal appearance is truly noble and majestic; being tall and well proportioned. His dress is a blue coat with buff-colored facings, a rich epaulette on each shoulder, buff under dress, and an elegant small sword; a black cockade in his hat.

Washington trained his army and kept a watchful eye on the movements of the British troops that occupied Boston. He decided the only way to drive the enemy out of the city would be to possess the high ground of Dorchester Heights. But his army did not have any cannons to use against them. Henry Knox, who had been a bookseller in Boston, led a daring expedition to Fort Ticonderoga, New York, to bring back the British artillery that had been captured there. Against all odds, Knox succeeded in hauling fifty-nine cannons over three hundred miles of ice and snow.

One morning in March 1776, the British troops woke up to a big surprise. They saw their own cannons on Dorchester Heights pointing down at them. Knowing the Americans had the advantage, they evacuated Boston on March 17, 1776. Boston was free of British control. Washington didn't know for sure where the British Army was going when they sailed out of Boston, but he suspected it would be New York. Manhattan Island and Long Island (with Brooklyn the westernmost point of Long Island) are separated by the Upper New York Bay and the East River. This was a strategic location because the army that controlled this area would have complete control over the ships entering and leaving New York Harbor as well as those sailing up and down the Hudson River. Washington decided that his Continental Army would get there first.

When they arrived in Manhattan, General Washington chose for his headquarters the Kennedy Mansion at Number One Broad Way (today's Broadway) near Fort George. The location gave the general an excellent view of New York Harbor, where Washington expected to see his enemy arrive any day.

King George III considered any colonist who opposed his rule a rebel, and he

THIS COMMANDER-IN-CHIEF FLAG flew over Washington's headquarters during the American Revolution. This flag with thirteen stars symbolized Washington's presence and authority. Today it is housed at the American Revolution Center.

intended to stop the rebellion. In a show of force, the king sent the British fleet—the most feared and most powerful navy in the world. In addition to his own professional soldiers, he paid Frederick II of Germany for the use of some of his men. Many of the Germans were from the Hesse-Cassel area and would become known as the Hessians.

Washington expected that King George would send his navy, so he began building defenses around the city of New York. At the end of June 1776, with their thin pendant flags fluttering in the breeze from the top of the tallest of their three wooden masts, the British fleet arrived in New York Harbor. The massive warships gathered around Staten Island, just off the tip of Manhattan. To the American patriots watching the buildup of ships and men, the wooden masts seemed as thick as a forest.

If the view out onto the harbor chilled the colonists' blood, they took heart in the news that arrived from Philadelphia. On July 9, 1776, Washington's troops gathered on the New York Commons (the area around the modern-day New York City Hall) to listen as the Declaration of Independence was read aloud.

Excited by the thought of independence, a mob of soldiers and citizens surged south down Broad Way. Their target was the statue of King George on a horse in the Bowling Green, near the tip of Manhattan. When they toppled the statue, they broke off the king's head. Then they cut off the king's nose and crown of laurels that encircled his head and put the noseless head on a spike. They proceeded back up Broad Way with their prize until they reached their favorite tavern. After planting the spike outside, they entered to celebrate. Ultimately, the rest of the King George statue was melted down—to make bullets to use against His Majesty's soldiers.

A few days later, the colonists had another largely symbolic encounter with their former king, this time between General Washington and Admiral Richard Howe of the British Royal Navy. Once again, a letter between warring armies would play a role in George Washington's life.

Admiral Howe anchored his flagship, the *Eagle*, in the harbor within sight of Washington's headquarters. On July 14, Admiral Howe sent men in a rowboat to the shore to deliver a letter to Washington.

IN JULY 1776, after listening to the Declaration of Independence, enthusiastic colonists toppled the statue of King George, which was located in the Bowling Green. They also knocked the decorative crowns off the fence posts. Today that fence, without the crowns, still encircles the Bowling Green at the end of Broadway in Manhattan.

As the enemy delegation approached the shore, Colonel Joseph Reed and Colonel Henry Knox, two of Washington's officers, met it.

"I have a letter, sir, from Lord Howe to Mr. Washington," said the captain of the *Eagle* after he bowed in a formal greeting.

Reed looked at the letter. It was addressed to "George Washington, Esq. New York"—Esq., or esquire, is a courtesy title.

Reed understood that the letter's address was an insult. By addressing it to "George Washington, Esq." Howe intentionally ignored Washington's position as commander in chief of the Continental Army. He should have addressed Washington as "his Excellency General George Washington."

"Sir, we have no person in our army with that address," said Reed.

"Sir, will you look at the address?" the British officer replied.

"No, sir, I cannot receive that letter."

Finally, the British officer asked what title should be used.

Colonel Reed asked him if he was aware of the "rank of General Washington in our army?"

The British officers boarded the boat and made their way back to the *Eagle* with the unopened letter.

Two days later, Reed and Knox met the boat again. This time the letter was addressed to "George Washington, Esq. and etc. etc." This too was an insult, as it still did not acknowledge Washington's rightful title. Reed refused to accept the letter.

> "Colonel Paterson appeared awe-struck, as if he was before something supernatural. Indeed, I don't wonder at it. He was before a very great man indeed."

The boat arrived again the next day, but this time there was no letter. The messenger asked if "His Excellency General Washington" would meet with James Patterson, the adjutant general of the British Army. The spoken message was relayed to His Excellency General Washington, who agreed to meet with him on July 20, 1776.

Henry Knox, who attended the meeting, had this to say: "General Washington was very handsomely dressed, and made a most elegant appearance. Colonel Paterson [James Patterson] appeared awe-struck, as if he was before something supernatural. Indeed, I don't wonder at it. He was before a very great man indeed."

James Patterson initially related that Admiral Howe regretted the mix-up over the address on the letters and explained that the "etc." implied "everything" that should follow. General Washington retorted that "etc." could also imply "anything." Using his genteel manners, General Washington explained to Colonel Patterson that he would not reply to any letter addressed to him as a private person when the issues related to his public position.

Patterson told Washington that there were discussions in Britain about granting pardons to American prisoners of war. General Washington politely explained to Patterson that if Americans were captured while defending their rights, they had done nothing wrong. And since they had done nothing wrong, they had no need for a pardon. Washington's bearing and manners helped him win a small battle over respect from his enemies, but it would prove small comfort as the year wore on.

Through the summer of 1776, General Washington watched the buildup of British forces on Staten Island. Thirty warships carried ten thousand trained sailors. Four hundred transport ships unloaded twenty-four thousand well-trained, well-fed professional soldiers. In stark contrast, Washington had fewer than nine thousand men in New York—none of whom were professional soldiers. They were schoolteachers, farmers, fishermen, some as young as fifteen, who had only used their guns to provide food for their families. Yet these poorly trained, poorly dressed, poorly fed patriots were prepared to fight professional British and Hessian soldiers to gain independence for America.

The Battle of Long Island began in Brooklyn on August 22, 1776. A week later, General Washington and his men were surrounded and outnumbered. The British soldiers, with their bayonets, were steadily digging a battle trench toward them. They were getting closer with each passing hour. Washington's army had to retreat from Brooklyn or be annihilated. Washington devised a daring escape plan to evacuate his men.

He ordered his troops to gather silently at the ferry landing, one group at a time. Washington supervised the retreat as boats ferried his men across the mile-wide East River to the safety of Manhattan. As the night dragged on, the soldiers who had not yet been evacuated were getting anxious and wondered what would happen at daybreak when the British troops could see them. Twenty-two-year-old Benjamin Tallmadge, an army officer, wrote about what happened next:

> When the dawn appeared there were
> several regiments still on duty. At this

time a very dense fog began to rise, and it seemed to settle in a peculiar manner over both encampments. I recollect this peculiar providential occurrence perfectly well; and so very dense was the atmosphere that I could scarcely discern a man at six yards' distance.

The fog made it impossible for the British to see the colonial retreat. Washington stayed to see that the last of his men were safely evacuated. Tallmadge wrote, "I think I saw Gen. Washington on the ferry stairs when I stepped into one of the last boats that received the troops."

Later that morning when the British could finally see the American camp, they were stunned. Like the fog—Washington's entire army had vanished. After the retreat from Brooklyn, Washington's men experienced one military defeat after another. They were forced to retreat from New York, then out of the colony of New York, and then out of the colony of New Jersey. By the end of the 1776, Washington's army had been pushed as far as Pennsylvania.

The Continental Army was in real trouble. At the beginning of the war, most soldiers had enlisted for short periods of time. Since the war was going badly, many left as soon as their enlistment commitment expired. At the beginning of December 1776, about half of Washington's men went home. He knew that the enlistment for many more would expire at the end of the month. General Washington had to do something fast to raise the morale of his men, or he would soon have no army to lead. David Ackerson, one of his commanders, recalled seeing General Washington at this time: "He was standing near a small camp-fire, evidently lost in thought and making no effort to keep warm. . . . His mouth was his strong feature, the lips being always tightly compressed. That day they were compressed so tightly as to be painful to look at."

General Washington chose his next move with care. A group of about fifteen hundred Hessians was stationed just across the Delaware River at Trenton, New Jersey. Washington planned to attack them before more of his men went home at the end of December. He chose December 25, hoping

the holiday might cause the Hessians to let down their guard a little bit.

After dark on Christmas Day, Washington's troops gathered on the banks of the Delaware. The weather had turned ugly. A mixture of rain, hail, and snow pelted the shivering men. The general hoped to have all of their cannons and equipment over the river by midnight. However, the ice chunks floating on the river and the falling snow hampered their movements. It was three in the morning before everything and everyone was safely across the freezing river. Washington led his twenty-four hundred men on a nine-mile march toward Trenton. They walked through the brutal weather in the predawn winter dark and finally arrived there at eight o'clock. The German mercenaries were surprised by the attack, but they quickly grabbed their nine-inch-tall brass caps and their guns and fought back.

General Washington personally led his men during the battle. Samuel Shaw wrote in his journal

ARTIST CHARLES WILLSON PEALE took part in the Battle of Trenton as a soldier under Washington's command. He later painted a portrait *(detail shown above left)* to commemorate the victory.

THIS CAP *(above right)* was worn by a member of a Hessian infantry unit during the American Revolution.

67

about how he and his fellow American soldiers felt about their general after the Battle of Trenton: "Our army love our General very much, but yet have one thing against him, which is the little care he takes of himself in any action. His personal bravery, and the desire he has of animating his troops by example, make him fearless of any danger."

Finally, Washington's men found out what victory in battle felt like. The next day, Washington congratulated his men for their "spirited and gallant behavior at Trenton." He knew that the enlistment for many of his men was about to expire, so he asked them not to "leave the business half finished at this important Crisis, a Crisis, which may, more than probably determine the fate of America." Even though his men were encouraged by their victory, many still planned to leave. On December 31, in a desperate effort to keep them, General Washington promised his soldiers a small bonus—if they would stay with him for just one more month. Some, but not all, of the soldiers agreed to stay that month to get the extra money.

In reality, Washington didn't have any bonus money to give them. He wrote Robert Morris, the man who controlled the finances for the war, to explain to him what he had done. Morris sent Washington the bonus money with a letter that said, "The year 1776 is over I am heartily glad of it & hope you nor America will ever be plagued with such another."

But the situation didn't look any better by the end of the next year. British troops occupied Philadelphia, which caused Congress to flee the capital city. The war had been going on for more than two years, and there was no end in sight. Some people thought George Washington was a complete failure in his role as commander in chief. Dr. James Craik, Washington's close friend and physician, warned him that "a Strong Faction was forming Against you in the New board of War and in the Congress."

For winter quarters, Washington chose a location less than twenty miles from Philadelphia—close enough to keep a watchful eye on the enemy yet far enough away to prevent a surprise attack. Snow covered the ground on December 19, 1777, as Washington, mounted on his horse Blueskin, led twelve thousand of his men into Valley Forge. As his position as commander in chief of the Continental Army required, General Washington was well-dressed in his buff and blue uniform. However, most of his men didn't have enough clothes to keep warm. Benjamin Tallmadge wrote about the condition of the regular soldiers: "Very few of them had a blanket to cover them. Indeed, the whole army were in great want of the most necessary articles of clothing, and many of them had no shoes to their feet, so that they could be traced by the blood which they left on the ground."

General Washington ordered his men to build themselves huts in which to live. While they were being built, the men suffered in the cold and slept in their canvas tents. General Washington was determined that he would endure the same conditions as his men. Instead of moving into the nearby home that served as his headquarters, Washington stayed in his own blue and white tent until his men had shelter too.

Even after two and a half years of war, his army did not have the basic needs. Washington began writing letters asking for supplies. On December 27, 1777, in a letter to Patrick Henry, then the governor of Virginia, Washington wrote that 2,898 men were "unfit for duty by reason of their being bare foot & otherwise naked."

> "...unfit for duty by reason of their being bare foot & otherwise naked."

His men had so few clothes among them that they began to pool them so that the man who was on duty in the freezing cold would have more to wear. Then when that man returned from duty, he would give the clothes to the next man on duty.

The Continental Army at Valley Forge was also hungry. Washington wrote a letter to New York's governor, George Clinton, on February 16, 1778, describing their situation,

"For some days past, there has been little less, than a famine in camp. A part of the army has been a week, without any kind of flesh & the rest three or four days. Naked and starving as they are, we cannot enough admire the incomparable patience and fidelity of the soldiery." How could he win a war if his own freezing soldiers didn't have enough to eat?

In addition to the lack of supplies, smallpox raged out of control, killing at least two thousand men. Since Washington had already had smallpox while in Barbados, he was immune.

Dr. James Thacher wrote, "This was the unhappy condition of the army, on whom General Washington had to relay for the defence of every thing held most dear by Americans, and this, too, while situated within sixteen miles of a powerful adversary, with a greatly superior army of veterans, watching with a vigilant eye for an opportunity to effect its destruction."

On February 23, 1778, Baron Friedrich Wilhelm Augustus von Steuben arrived at Valley Forge. He had served in the Prussian Army and as an aide-de-camp under Frederick II, the king of Prussia.

After completing his service, von Steuben searched for another way to use his military knowledge. He met Benjamin Franklin in France and decided to offer his services to General Washington.

Von Steuben set to work immediately adapting European war drills to the needs of the American troops. Although the Continental Army was poorly equipped, von Steuben found two valuable assets the Americans had that no other country did. One thing was perseverance. Some soldiers deserted to the British in Philadelphia to ease their desperate situation, but many young men like Joseph Plumb Martin determined that they were "engaged in the defence of our injured country and were willing, nay, we were determined to persevere." The other valuable American asset was General George Washington. After meeting Washington the first time, von Steuben's aide, Pierre-Etienne Duponceau, described his impressions:

> I could not keep my eyes from that imposing countenance; grave, yet not severe; affable, without familiarity.

Its predominant expression was calm dignity, through which you could trace the strong feelings of the patriot, and discern the father, as well as the commander of his soldiers. I have never seen a picture, that represents him to me, as I saw him at Valley-Forge, and during the campaign in which I had the honour to follow him. Perhaps that expression was beyond the skill of the painter; but while I live it will remain impressed on my memory.

Valley Forge proved to be a turning point not only for the Continental Army but also for George Washington. A committee of congressmen arrived to check on the leadership of General Washington. They saw for themselves the desperate condition of the troops. They also understood that Washington refused to publicly defend himself against his critics because he didn't want their enemies to know how desperate the situation was at Valley Forge. If the British knew their weaknesses, they would attack and defeat them. By the time the congressional committee left Valley Forge, they completely supported General George Washington. They knew no one could ever replace him.

> **"I could not keep my eyes from that imposing countenance; grave, yet not severe; affable, without familiarity."**

General Washington fought alongside of his men and suffered with his men. In return, they adored him and followed him without question. When George Washington became commander in chief of the Continental Army, he risked everything he had: his family, his home, his reputation, his country, and his life. If the American patriots lost the war, Washington would lose everything he held dear.

CHAPTER SEVEN

WASHINGTON AT FORTY-FIVE

Sitting astride his horse Blueskin at Valley Forge, General Washington couldn't have known that before the war was over he would lose most of his battles, many of his men, and some of his teeth. And he never would have imagined that more than 225 years later, he and his horse would be reunited.

FACE OF A LEADER

At Valley Forge, during the winter of 1777–1778, the weight of responsibility for the Continental Army rested on Washington's shoulders. He likely felt the strain from the difficult past year and was concerned about the future and resolved to persevere.

Stuart Williamson created a sculpture that suggested the burden Washington must have felt, putting puckers between his eyes and creases at the corners. He studied the Houdon bust and applied his knowledge of how some tooth loss affects the face. He made the skin on the face of the forty-five-year-old man slightly loose. He also added the smallpox scar on his left cheek that had not been present when he sculpted the face of Washington as a teenager. Williamson created a look on General Washington's face that reveals both tension and determination.

After the wax replica of this clay head was ready, Williamson added acrylic eyeballs to General Washington, whose pupils were the same blue-gray color

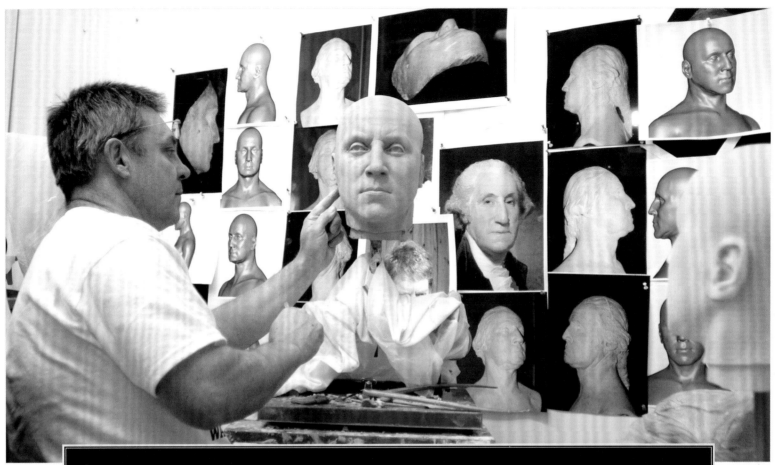

STUART WILLIAMSON, shown here working on General Washington, kept portraits and photographs of the Houdon mask and bust close at hand while he sculpted.

they used for Washington at nineteen. The only difference was the whites of the eyes. When this set was made, red silk threads were added to the whites to give them a bloodshot look. When Williamson placed these realistic-looking eyeballs into the head, General Washington looked as if he was tired and weary.

Sue Day again painted layer after layer to produce a surface that looks like real skin with the normal spots and freckles that would have resulted after years in the sun. Knowing Washington's pale skin would have been red in the cold weather at Valley Forge, Day painted tiny, red veins on his cheeks.

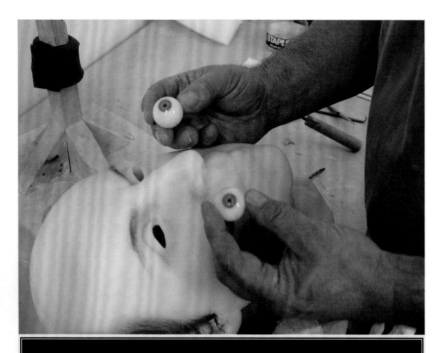

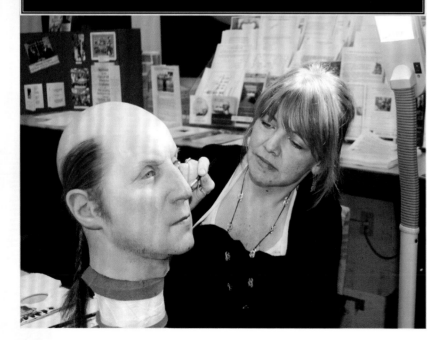

WILLIAMSON PREPARES to place the eyeballs in the wax head of Washington *(above)*.

SUE DAY TOUCHES UP the paint on Washington's face *(below)*.

Some gray was showing in General Washington's hair at this point in his life. To reflect this, Day and Horak used the original reddish-brown hair color and mixed some gray hairs into it as they worked. Day inserted hair at the back of his head and at his temples and sideburns but didn't insert hair on the top of his head because the figure of General Washington would be wearing a hat. Horak made the hair on the wig begin at about the middle of his head. When the hair was finished, Horak styled the general's hair in a queue using a simple black ribbon.

For the eyebrows, Day added a few gray hairs into the color mix. She made them thinner than they were when he was a teenager but kept the same shape. One by one, she placed eyelashes into General Washington's eyelids, as she did for each figure.

GEORGE WASHINGTON'S WHITE HORSE

The Mount Vernon exhibit of Washington at Valley Forge would depict the general astride Blueskin. James Rees and Ann Bay had a clear idea of how they wanted Blueskin to look. They wanted his physical position to convey that he was a strong horse—but also tired from a long year at war.

StudioEIS contacted Frank J. Zitz and Company, a design and taxidermy studio, to re-create this famous horse. Zitz produces high-quality, lifelike reproductions of animals that are used in museums, stores, and private collections. Zitz uses the hides of real animals for his exhibits. To create an authentic reproduction of Blueskin, Zitz needed to find the right horse. Blueskin was a blue roan. This type of horse has dark skin and white hair. In the summer, when the hair of a blue roan is short, the animal appears to be a bluish color. In the winter, when the hair grows longer, a blue roan appears to be white. Zitz located a blue roan on an Amish farm in Pennsylvania that had come to the end of his long life as a farm animal. When the horse died, its hide was removed and tanned to preserve the skin for later use.

The figure of General Washington had to look natural on Blueskin's back. To ensure this, Elliot Schwartz took pictures of a man similar to Washington's size and shape sitting on horseback. His pictures allowed his fellow artists at StudioEIS to see how a real body is positioned while sitting in a saddle.

Zitz completed the form of Blueskin's back, from shoulder to hips, and sent it to StudioEIS. Once there, a man sat on the back of the form, and a plaster cast was made of the lower half of his body. This cast was incorporated into the lower half of the body of General Washington to ensure a perfect fit between the general and his horse. The body form of Washington had to be designed so his clothing could be taken on and off. The finished form of Washington's body was covered in plaster and sealed. When StudioEIS was finished with Blueskin's back, they returned it to Zitz.

Zitz took the section of Blueskin's back and fitted it onto a steel frame. The frame was necessary to support the heavy figure. From there, Zitz added pieces of a horse-shaped mannequin made of foam. When this phase was complete, he had a complete horse made of foam.

Next, Zitz used clay to add details such as veins and muscles to the face and the legs of the foam horse.

The next step was to cover the horse form with the tanned hide of the real blue roan horse. The horse's hide was rehydrated and fit onto the form using glue. It was sewn together underneath the form. On the areas of the horse where the skin shows, such as around the eyes, the ears, and the nose, Zitz used an airbrush to paint on layers of color to create a realistic look. The mane and the tail of the horse were sparse, so hair extensions were added to make them appear fuller. A cast of the teeth from a real horse was used to create a set of synthetic teeth for Blueskin. Finally, Blueskin got a set of glass eyes.

Craftspeople from the harness shop at Colonial Williamsburg made the various pieces of tack—the equipment used to ride a horse—by hand, using eighteenth-century methods. The choices Washington made about his equipment and his tack—like the clothing he chose for himself—were functional and fashionable. To re-create authentic objects, they studied lists of supplies Washington ordered from a saddle maker as well as life portraits of the general that included his horse.

Jim Kladder made the bridle and also the bearskin holster holder that held Washington's pistol. The general's choice of a holster made from bearskin was practical—bearskin would stand up to hard use—but it also looked ferocious. Stuart Lilie made the housing, or saddle cloth, out of mohair plush material that was light brown and trimmed in a gold color. Jimmy Leach made Washington's plain English-style hunting saddle. The handmade saddle took Kladder about a month of workdays to complete. With all his riding gear complete, Blueskin was ready for his rider.

THE MAN MADE THE CLOTHES

Clothing worn by General Washington gave researchers additional clues about the size and shape of his body, as well as his posture. Authentic articles of clothing worn by Washington have been preserved in several U.S. museums including Mount Vernon, the Smithsonian Institution,

Morristown National Historic Park, and the Chicago History Museum.

Textile expert Linda Baumgarten studied Washington's clothes. She and the other conservators who assisted her measured the garments and made notes about the fabric, details, and any damage. Most of the surviving articles were worn by Washington during his presidency. However, the breeches and waistcoat on display at the Smithsonian Institution were worn by the general during the American Revolution. From his clothing, Baumgarten confirmed that Washington had long, thin arms; his chest would have measured about 41 to 42 inches; his waist, about 35 to 37 inches; and his thighs, 20 to 22 inches. She estimated that if George Washington bought a suit today, the jacket would be a size 42 long and the length of his shirtsleeve would be

37 or 38 inches. When the measurements of Washington's actual clothes were compared to Houdon's life-sized statue, they matched.

Baumgarten supplied the measurements and notes she took to tailor Henry Cooke. But Cooke knew that the measurements alone didn't tell him how Washington's body mass would have been distributed inside the clothes. For that, he too needed to see the garments himself. Cooke calls clothes "a mold of the human body which lies beneath them." Wear patterns on the clothes would show him the true shape of Washington's body, not just the size.

Using Washington's clothing to determine his true size and shape was reliable since his clothes were custom-made by a tailor. According to Cooke, the fit of Washington's clothing was "close but without constraint." The reason for this tight fit goes beyond what was fashionable. At this point in time, the type of clothing people wore was a good indicator about their station in life. Cooke explained, "For one who worked as a laborer, their clothes would have been cut broader and wider for more ease as they worked." But as a member of the gentry class, Washington's clothes were

meant to "enhance the ease and elegance" of the wearer and would have "fit close to the chest, shoulder and arms," reinforcing proper posture at all times. The sleeves of a gentleman's coat were constructed to have a "crooked" elbow so that when he stood properly—with his arms at his sides and bent slightly—the sleeve of his coat would lie flat. The shoulders of the coat were set in place in a way that would keep his shoulders pulled back and down in a rounded shape. Knee breeches, which stopped just below the knee, fit close to the knee and the leg but had fullness in the seat to allow him to sit and ride a horse.

In addition to his surviving garments, a lot of information about Washington's body comes from his own letters. Before the American Revolution, Washington—like most colonial gentlemen—ordered his clothes from tailors in London. He was keenly aware of British fashion, and his descriptions of the clothes he wanted were precise and direct. In a letter to his tailor Charles Lawrence on October 24, 1763, he requested, "a suit of Cloaths made of superfine broad Cloth, and as light as possible for Summer wear—I have seen them made of light coloured mixed

Cloths without linings, bound holes &ca [etc.] which is handsome enough—one of these kind you may send, or of any other sort that is more in taste as the fashions are often changing." Since Washington was not the size of a typical man, many of his letters to tailors were filled with complaints about the fit of the clothes they sent him. In another letter to Charles Lawrence on June 20, 1768, Washington writes,

> As I have sent you my measure once or twice I presume you can be at no loss for want of one but I think you have generally sent my Cloaths too short & sometimes too tight for which Reason I think it necessary again to mention that I am full Six feet high which may be a good direction to you as to the length and as I am not at all inclind to be corpulent you might easily come at my size even if your measure of me shoud be lost—let the Breeches be made long.

Henry Cooke combined all this information to develop the patterns he used to make the general's clothing in the correct size. To determine the style of the general's coat, Cooke studied the uniform at the Smithsonian Institution. He took meticulous notes and made sketches that he used to re-create the coat down to the smallest details. The color Cooke used for the general's clothes were based on his authentic uniform and the portraits of Washington painted by Charles Willson Peale that depicted him in 1777 and 1778.

> "...you have generally sent my Cloaths too short & sometimes too tight for which Reason I think it necessary again to mention that I am full Six feet high..."

Cooke used modern fabrics of the same type that were available historically to construct the clothes. The blue woolen cloth used for the uniform coat and cape is the same fabric used today inside a Rolls-Royce automobile. Cooke used a sewing

machine to construct the inside parts of the garments, but every visible stitch and finishing detail was done by hand. The work was time consuming. The uniform coat alone took Cooke about eighty hours to complete.

Cooke arranged for other craftspeople to make some pieces of General Washington's clothing. Washington's knee breeches were made from leather, and they would not have been made by a tailor but by a specialist in leatherwork. Cooke contacted Jay Howlett, a leather craftsman, to do the job. Howlett drafted his own pattern by considering the measurements of Washington's existing breeches and by studying leather breeches in other historic clothing collections. He also had to keep in mind that the leather breeches must later be pulled onto the inflexible model of Washington's body—with his legs outstretched on his horse.

THIS UNIFORM COAT, waistcoat, and breeches are on display at the Smithsonian Institution, Museum of American History. Washington wore the waistcoat and breeches during the American Revolution and the uniform coat when he was president. Measurements from clothing worn by Washington were used to determine the size and shape of his body.

Howlett made the breeches out of high-quality elk skins ordered from a German company that makes lederhosen. The breeches took him about fifty hours to complete. Then he had a friend wear them around for a couple of days. This broke the leather in enough to establish the seat and the knees. The man rode a horse and wiped his hands on his thighs to give the breeches a realistic, lived-in look.

Howlett also made the hat worn by General Washington, choosing the style based on portraits of him and other officers of the day.

When Neal Hurst made the shirt worn by General Washington, he considered the style that was in fashion for men's shirts at the time. Although the basic shape of the shirt was the same, the collar was larger than those worn when Washington was a teen. Even at war, Washington would have dressed as a gentleman, complete with a linen shirt that had ruffles down the front and at the sleeves. Hurst made countless precise hand stitches to create the historically accurate shirt.

General Washington would have worn leather gloves while riding his horse—and fortunately some of his gloves still exist. Mark Hutter, another craftsman specializing in eighteenth-century clothing, was called in to re-create them. StudioEIS provided Hutter with a plaster mold of the model's hands made in the desired position to depict Washington holding a horse's reins in the left hand and the right hand resting on top. Hutter spent many hours studying the construction techniques of Washington's gloves and other gloves from the eighteenth century to develop a pattern he could use to re-create historically accurate gloves that would fit the hands sent by StudioEIS. It took Hutter ten hours to sew the sheepskin gloves, and when he was done, the gloves fit the figure of General Washington's hands perfectly.

In the eighteenth century, footwear was not made for a right foot and a left foot. Both were made exactly the same, and wearers molded them to their feet. Ken Treese made Washington's boots and shoes using this historically accurate method. For General Washington, Treese made high-top black leather boots. The pair took more than thirty hours to make by hand. Treese had a man with feet of the right size wear the boots to make them appear used.

The figure of forty-five-year-old General Washington was finished. He was dressed and placed on the back of his horse Blueskin, looking as he did at Valley Forge. The look on his face shows the burden he must have felt. He and his men had endured more than two years of war already, and the end was nowhere in sight. As commander in chief, he was responsible for the hungry men who had walked into camp leaving bloody footprints behind them. Both the general and his men believed the price of independence was worth the cost.

GENERAL GEORGE WASHINGTON as he would have looked at the age of forty-five

CHAPTER EIGHT

BECOMING PRESIDENT WASHINGTON

While American troops were training at Valley Forge, Benjamin Franklin was in Paris negotiating with the French. On February 6, 1778, Franklin and his fellow diplomats signed the Treaty of Alliance. This treaty between Louis XVI, the king of France, and the United States of America formed a military agreement against Great Britain. In response to this treaty, on June 18, 1778, the British troops who had occupied Philadelphia abandoned the city and marched toward New York.

The next day, General Washington led his army out of Valley Forge to pursue the enemy. The military training his Continental Army received from von Steuben was put to the test on June 28 at the Battle of Monmouth. Soon after the fighting began, Washington encountered some soldiers who were retreating. When he asked them why, he found out that General Charles Lee, his second in command, had ordered a retreat (for his actions, Lee was later court-martialed, found guilty, and forced out of the army). Washington was shocked at the news. He stopped their retreat, rallied his men, and led them into battle. Marquis de Lafayette, a young Frenchman who became like a son to Washington, described how the general looked that day as he took control of the chaos. Lafayette wrote that Washington was "mounted on a splendid charger, rode along the ranks amid the shouts of the soldiers, cheering them by his voice and example, and restoring to our standard the fortunes of the fight. I thought then as now, that never had I seen so superb a man." Although neither side was a clear winner in the battle, it proved that the Continental Army had become a fighting force that was equal to the professional British soldiers.

General Washington continued to lead his men into battle as the war dragged on year after year. Although the Continental Army lost more battles than it won, the soldiers always managed to survive to fight another day. And then came a turning point.

In 1781 France agreed to send some naval vessels and additional soldiers to assist General Washington. When the French generals and their officers met him, they were impressed by his abilities as commander in chief. Abbé Robin, a chaplain in the French army, wrote on August 4, 1781, that Washington could

> impress upon his soldiers an absolute subordination, to make them eager to deserve his praise, to make them fear even his silence, to keep up their

confidence even after defeats, to gain the most glorious reputation and obtain the most extensive powers without arousing envy or creating suspicion, . . . never to have more reserves than when they seemed to be exhausted; never more fiercely to strike the enemy than after been defeated; to stimulate the enthusiasm of the least enthusiastic of all peoples; . . . fearless in the midst of dangers, but seeking danger only when the good of the country was at stake.

> "I thought then as now that never had I seen so superb a man."

General Washington's reputation with the French army had certainly improved since his experience at Fort Necessity when the French had considered him no better than an assassin.

The place where the French navy could be used to the best advantage was against Lord Charles Cornwallis in Yorktown, Virginia, near Williamsburg. As General Washington traveled south toward Yorktown, he would pass by Mount Vernon. He had not been home in six years, since May 1775 when he rode away to attend the Second Continental Congress. On September 9, 1781, Washington rode his horse through the gate at the far end of the pasture and saw his own beloved Mount Vernon. He stayed at Mount Vernon for three days, as he and the French generals discussed plans for the battle in Yorktown.

In Yorktown, on October 6, General Washington ceremoniously struck a pickax into the ground as a signal for his troops to begin digging the battle trenches. When the advance work was ready, the soldiers were told not to begin firing their cannons until they saw the signal—the raising of the American flag. Joseph Plumb Martin wrote,

About noon the much wished for signal went up. I confess I felt a secret pride swell my heart when I saw the "star spangled banner" waving majestically in the very faces of our implacable adversaries; it appeared like an omen of success to our enterprise, and so it proved in reality. A simultaneous discharge of all the guns in the line followed; the French troops accompanying it with "Huzza for the Americans!"

The battle continued day after day until British commander Lord Cornwallis was beaten and he knew it. On October 17, he suggested they discuss terms of surrender.

The surrender ceremony took place two days later on a beautiful autumn afternoon. Crowds of people from the area came to watch. The French band played music as the French soldiers lined the left side of the lane, dressed in their best uniforms. American soldiers lined the right side, dressed in their tattered, battle-worn clothes. The line of soldiers stretched out more than a mile. James Thacher noted that the face of every American soldier "beamed with satisfaction and joy."

On that day, General Washington chose to ride his horse Nelson, a chestnut horse with a white face and legs, instead of Blueskin. Nelson had carried the general during many battles because Nelson stayed calmer in the midst of the noise and chaos of battle than did Blueskin. George Washington, the victorious general, waited for Lord Cornwallis at the head of the Continental army. By Washington's side was the long, thin sword with a green handle he carried with him throughout the war.

When the lead British officer, Charles O'Hara, arrived where Washington waited, he explained that Lord Cornwallis was too ill to attend and that he, Cornwallis's second in command, would surrender the sword of General Cornwallis. O'Hara proceeded to hand over the sword to the French commander but was told that it should be surrendered to Washington instead. When O'Hara tried to present Cornwallis's sword to General Washington, Washington politely pointed toward Major General Benjamin Lincoln—Washington's second in command. Everyone understood his meaning. This breach of propriety, like the long-ago letter in New York that had been addressed to Mr. George Washington, would not be tolerated.

As it turned out, the Battle of Yorktown was the last major battle of the American

Revolution. However, the war wasn't over until two years later when the final peace treaty was signed on September 3, 1783.

British troops, who had occupied New York City since 1776, planned to evacuate on November 25, 1783. On that day, they left the British Union Jack flag flying on the flagpole at Fort George until the very last minute. When they finally took it down, as a final insult, they sabotaged the pulley and greased the flagpole. An American patriot responded quickly as he gathered a hammer, nails, and boards, and used them to climb to the top of the slippery flagpole. He hung the American flag whose stars and stripes represented the thirteen colonies that were now free and independent from the British king.

General George Washington waited on his horse outside the city. As soon as the last British soldier departed from the tip of Manhattan—but before their ships had cleared the American harbor—General Washington made his public entrance into the city.

He left New York City in defeat. He returned in victory.

General Washington's work was over, and it was time to go home. He invited his officers to meet with him one last time before he left the city. At noon on December 4, Washington walked down Pearl Street and entered Fraunces Tavern. He climbed the stairs to the Long Room, where his men stood on the wide plank floor, waiting in an uneasy silence.

Some of them had been with Washington since the war began at the Siege of Boston. For the past eight years, they had been a family. They ate together, traveled together, plotted battles together, and fought the enemy together.

"With a heart full of love and gratitude, I now take leave of you. I most devoutly wish that your latter days may be as prosperous and happy as your former ones have been glorious and honorable," said General Washington as he lifted his wineglass to offer a toast. They drank to his toast.

"I cannot come to each of you, but shall feel obliged if each of you will come and take me by the hand," General Washington said.

General Henry Knox, who was standing closest to him, turned to his commander, his general, and his friend. Washington's blue-gray eyes were full of tears. Knox took

WASHINGTON SAID GOOD-BYE to his officers in this room at Fraunces Tavern on December 4, 1783. The building still stands today in lower Manhattan and is open for visitors.

him by the hand. They embraced. Both of them wept. Neither one could speak. When Knox stepped away, another officer came to take his place. One by one, each weeping officer came to General Washington to shake his hand and embrace him.

As Benjamin Tallmadge said good-bye to Washington, he knew it was unlikely that he would ever see him again since the general would return to Virginia and he to Connecticut. Tallmadge wrote about how he and his fellow officers felt: "The simple

thought that we were then about to part from the man who conducted us through a long and bloody war, and under whose conduct the glory and independence of our country had been achieved, and that we should see his face no more in this world, seemed to me utterly insupportable."

As Washington left Fraunces Tavern, a group of infantry soldiers stood at attention so their general and his officers could walk through them. A huge crowd followed Washington down the cobblestone street as he walked to the nearby wharf where a barge waited for him.

He climbed in, and the crew pushed out into the East River. Every eye was on their beloved general. As a sign of respect, Washington took off his hat and waved it at the watching crowd. Every man onshore removed his hat in return.

General Washington went directly to Annapolis, Maryland, where Congress was meeting. On December 22, the governor hosted a celebration ball at the Maryland State House. Fifty-one-year-old Washington danced every dance because most of the ladies in attendance wanted to "get a touch of him." The years of war had not changed his dancing ability or his manners as a gentleman.

The next day, Washington appeared before Congress and a full house of spectators to retire his commission as commander in chief. Since he was not a good public speaker, he had written down what he wanted to say. His hand shook as he read his remarks from the page. When he reached the part where he spoke about his family of military officers who had been with him during the war, the paper in his hand shook even harder. He reached up

with his other hand to steady the paper. As their beloved general struggled to control his emotions, members of Congress and the rest of the crowd wept openly.

"Having now finished the work assigned me, I retire from the great theatre of Action—and bidding an Affectionate farewell to this August body under whose orders I have so long acted, I here offer my Commission, and take my leave of all the employments of public life," he said in a strong, clear voice.

Washington handed his commission papers to the president of the Congress. The job he'd taken on in 1775 was finished. All Washington wanted to do was eat Christmas dinner in his own home.

Mount Vernon was covered with a bright white blanket of snow when Washington rode through the gate the next day. It was Christmas Eve. He was delighted to be home and got acquainted with the newest residents of Mount Vernon, his step-grandchildren four-year-old Nelly and two-year-old Wash (George Washington Parke Custis). After the death of their father, Jacky Custis, they came to live with their grandmother, Martha Washington.

WASHINGTON DESIGNED THIS outhouse in the years between the American Revolution and his presidency as part of a major renovation of Mount Vernon. The door at the bottom of the outhouse opened up, which allowed the tray to be emptied.

In the eight and a half years Washington had been away at war, his home and eight-thousand-acre farm had deteriorated. Now that he was home, his thoughts shifted from war to ways to improve the function and beauty of his home, gardens, and farm. He added flagstone to the piazza that stretched across the length of the house. He also added a graceful walk through the trees he had planted on each side of the bowling green, and he planted gardens enclosed by a brick wall. Within the garden wall, Washington designed unique "necessaries" (outhouses) that had removable drawers beneath the seats.

He sought ways to improve his farming methods and devised a seven-year crop rotation plan to prevent the soil's nutrients from being depleted. He experimented with different types of fertilizers, including creek mud, fish heads, animal manure, and even the human waste collected from the drawers of the "necessaries."

Washington learned that mules (the offspring of a male donkey and a female horse) made more efficient farm animals than horses. He soon received several donkeys from Europe and became the foremost person in North America to promote the breeding of mules.

Although Washington had retired from public life, he was still a famous person. Visitors flocked to Mount Vernon. Some, like Jean-Antoine Houdon and his assistants, were invited. But many were strangers who dropped by to meet George Washington. All were welcomed with warm hospitality.

No matter how many visitors were at his home, Washington kept to his usual schedule. He got up before five o'clock and descended the private staircase that connected the hall outside his bedroom to the hall outside his study. He ducked as he got to the bottom of the stair because he was taller than the opening. In his study, he read letters and answered them. At exactly seven, he drank tea and ate Indian hoecakes with butter and honey. Then he rode out on horseback to inspect his farms and the work of his slaves and employees. Sometimes the circuit would take him over fifteen miles. He returned to the front door promptly at a quarter to three, dismounted and, with a flick of the whip, the horse he'd trained himself trotted off to the stable unattended.

Washington then dressed for dinner, which was served precisely at three. He stayed at the dinner table for an hour to visit with his family. Later in the evening, after tea time, if they did not have overnight guests, he would return to his study to work. He went to bed at nine. His schedule varied only on Sunday, when the Washingtons often attended church and then enjoyed a day of rest. On Sunday evenings, George would read to Martha and the grandchildren from a book of sermons or from sacred writings.

While Washington's home and farm was stable and serene, his country was not. During the war, the thirteen colonies joined together to defeat their common enemy. Now that they were independent, they had to fashion a government that suited their new situation.

The thirteen states faced many difficult questions. Who would pay the remaining war debts? Who would control navigation on the vital Mississippi River? Who would control the western wilderness? Would national rights be more important than the rights of each state? Should slavery be allowed to continue?

Each state was only concerned about the needs of its own people, with no regard for the other twelve states. The Articles of Confederation, signed on March 1, 1781, gave Congress no power to enforce any decisions. The United States was in serious trouble and seemed to be falling apart. If things didn't change, a foreign power might try to take control of the United States. If that happened, six years of war would have been pointless.

Washington was worried the fragile new nation might not survive until a new system of government was established. In a letter to James Madison on November 5, 1786, Washington wrote that unless there was a change, the country they had spent years trying to form "at the expence of much blood and treasure, must fall. We are fast verging to anarchy & confusion!" He believed the only hope for the future was for the states to band together to form a strong central government.

A convention in Philadelphia was planned to discuss the issues. On December 6, 1786, Edmund Randolph, Virginia's governor, wrote Washington to tell him that he had been appointed to be one of the delegates from their state and added, "The gloomy prospect still admits one ray of hope, that those, who began, carried on & Consummated the revolution, can yet rescue America from the impending ruin."

> "The gloomy prospect still admits one ray of hope, that those, who began, carried on & Consummated the revolution, can yet rescue America from the impending ruin."

Although fifty-five-year-old Washington was deeply concerned about the state of affairs, he did not want to go to Philadelphia as a delegate and wrote Randolph to explain his reasons. At the time, Washington was suffering from a painful shoulder saying, "I am hardly able to raise my hand to my head or turn myself in bed." Another factor was that when he announced his

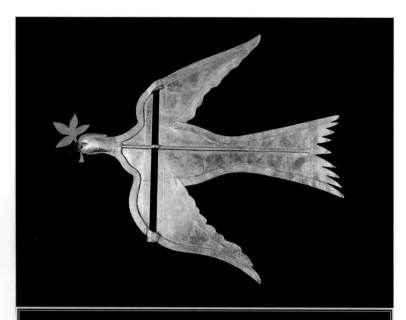

in the shape of a dove of peace that Washington ordered while he was in Philadelphia to attend the Constitutional Convention. It was placed on top of the cupola at Mount Vernon, where it stayed until 1993, when it was removed to protect it from the elements. Today an exact replica has replaced it.

cause to charge my conduct with inconsistency, in again appearing on a public theater after a public declaration to the contrary; and because it will, I fear, have a tendency to sweep me back into the tide of public affairs, when retirement and ease is so essentially necessary for, and is so much desired by me.

Even though Washington preferred to stay home, ultimately he agreed to go as a delegate. He and his men sacrificed for eight years, and many good men died in battle to gain independence from Britain. His country needed him, and Washington would not allow it to collapse.

Washington traveled once again to Philadelphia as a delegate to Congress. In 1775, the last time he was a congressional delegate, they had discussed how to become an independent nation. This time they would discuss how best to govern that new nation.

When the fifty-five delegates to Congress convened on May 25, 1787, the first order of business was to decide who would preside over the meeting. By unanimous vote, Washington, the man respected by

retirement from public life as he resigned his commission as commander in chief to Congress, he meant it. He wrote,

It is not only inconvenient for me to leave home, but because there will be, I apprehend, too much everyone, was elected to be the president of the convention. They planned to revise the Articles of Confederation. However, as they discussed the issues, it became clear to all that only a new document would satisfy the new nation's needs.

Long and angry debates raged for up to seven hours a day about how the new government should work. All through the sweltering summer the windows of the Pennsylvania State House stayed closed so no one could overhear the discussions. By the end of the summer, they had created a system of government—run by the people—that was radically different from any other in the world at the time. It would have three different branches—the legislative, the judicial, and the executive. Each would work with the others, but none would have too much power. And they created and defined the offices of the president and the vice president.

They wrote down an outline of the basic principles for their new government in a document. On September 17, 1787, the delegates were ready to sign the agreement, which they called the Constitution.

The American Revolution freed the thirteen colonies from Britain. The Constitution united thirteen independent states and created one nation. George Washington was given the honor of being the first man to sign the Constitution. That night he wrote in his journal that he returned to his lodgings "to meditate on the momentous [work] which had been executed."

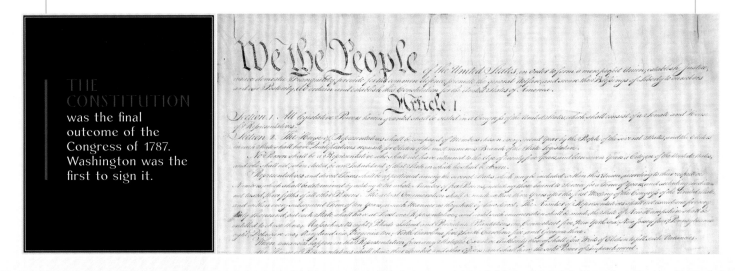

THE CONSTITUTION was the final outcome of the Congress of 1787. Washington was the first to sign it.

A year after the Constitution was signed, Congress established the workings of the new government. Many issues—such as where the capital would be located, how the senators and representatives would be elected, and the details for the first presidential election—had to be discussed and settled.

Immediately, newspapers across the country as well as his friends suggested that George Washington should be president. Washington didn't encourage this thinking at all.

At the time, David Humphreys, a former aide-de-camp to the general during the war, was living at Mount Vernon while working on a biography of George Washington. According to Humphreys, Washington said,

> God knows that I have but one wish myself, which is to live & die on my own plantation. It is said that every man has his portion of ambition. I may have mine I suppose as well as the rest; but if I know my own heart, my ambition would not lead me into public life; my only ambition is to do my duty in this world as well as I am capable of performing it, & to merit the good opinion of all good men.

Humphreys wrote that because of a variety of considerations and correspondence, the "General became convinced that it was his indispensable duty to accept the Presidency."

•••

As the time for the election drew closer, it seemed likely that he would be elected president. He told Humphreys, "I feel very much like a man who is condemned to death does when the time of his execution draws nigh." Once again, George Washington was torn between his desire to stay home and duty to his country.

About noon on April 14, 1789, the secretary of Congress, Charles Thomson, arrived at Mount Vernon. He announced that George Washington had been "elected to the office of President of the United States of America." He had received a unanimous vote.

Two days later, George Washington left for New York, the temporary capital of the country. Martha and their grandchildren would come later. Washington wrote in his journal, "About ten o'clock I bade adieu to Mount Vernon, to private life, and to domestic felicity; and with a mind oppressed with more anxious and painful sensations than I have words to express, set out for New York."

Washington understood that as the first president, everything he did would be watched and noted. To his inauguration, he wanted to wear a suit made from fabric produced in the United States. Most of the clothing and fabric used in the United States was imported from Britain and France. He wanted to send the message that from this point forward, the United States of America would begin producing its own goods. The Woolen Manufactory at Hartford, Connecticut, succeeded in producing some high-quality broadcloth fabric and gave it to Washington. A tailor created his inaugural suit out of this brown fabric.

On April 30, 1789, Inauguration Day events began at nine o'clock in the morning when every church in the city held a

THE OLD FEDERAL HALL as it looked when Washington stood on the second-story balcony and took the oath of office as the first president of the United States.

prayer service on behalf of the nation, the president, and the vice president. Following this, every member of Congress took his place at Federal Hall. To witness the historic event, crowds of people packed the intersection of Wall and Broad streets and peeked out from every window and rooftop as they waited.

At noon the hooves of six white horses clattered on the cobblestones of Wall Street as they pulled a white coach carrying one man. Fifty-seven-year-old George Washington climbed out. Out of respect, the silent crowd removed their hats, and Washington removed his. He bowed to the right and left as he moved through the masses of people. Nearing the building, he walked through a line of soldiers and was escorted inside and took a seat in a mahogany armchair. Vice President John Adams told Washington that members of Congress would accompany him as he took the oath of office.

So more people could witness the ceremony, the oath of office would take place on the second-floor balcony, which had been decorated with red and white striped bunting. Federal Hall had recently been remodeled using patriotic symbols. On the balcony, the middle wrought-iron railing featured a design of thirteen arrows, representing the thirteen states. The pediment above featured the image of an eagle.

Washington stepped onto the balcony wearing a ceremonial sword and dressed in the height of fashion. He wore a linen shirt with pleated ruffles underneath his suit. His waistcoat and jacket were made of the same brown fabric as his knee breeches. For this formal occasion, his hair was pulled back in a braid, covered in white powder, and then tucked into a black silk bag.

Robert Livingston, the chancellor of the State of New York, administered the oath of office. Secretary of the Senate Samuel Otis held a huge Bible.

Washington placed his hand on the Bible and said: "I do solemnly swear that I will faithfully execute the office of President of the United States, and will to the best of my ability, preserve, protect and defend the Constitution of the United States."

Livingston raised the Bible slightly, and Washington bent over and kissed it.

"Long live George Washington, the President of the United States!" exclaimed Livingston when he turned to the crowd.

"Huzza! Huzza! Huzza!" roared the masses.

President George Washington bowed.

"Huzza! Huzza! Huzza!" they cheered.

Some were so overcome with emotion that they could not speak. Tears of joy rolled down the cheeks of many members of Congress and people in the crowd.

At that moment, a U.S. flag was hoisted up the flagpole on the roof directly above the balcony. Soldiers stationed at the southern tip of Manhattan finally saw the signal they had been waiting for. When they saw the stars and stripes flying over Federal Hall, they began a thirteen-cannon salute. The rumble of cannon fire once again shook New York City—this time to celebrate the first president of the United States.

Dignitaries from other countries were in the crowd that day. Comte de Moustier, a representative from France, described George Washington by saying, "He has the soul, look, and figure of a hero united in him. Born to command, he never seems embarrassed with the homage rendered him, and he has the advantage of mingling great dignity with great simplicity of manner."

The day made history. The people of America had fought and won their independence from Britain. They had created a new nation with a new form of government. And they had chosen their own leader: President George Washington.

WASHINGTON'S SIGNATURE on the bottom of his inaugural address, delivered April 30, 1789

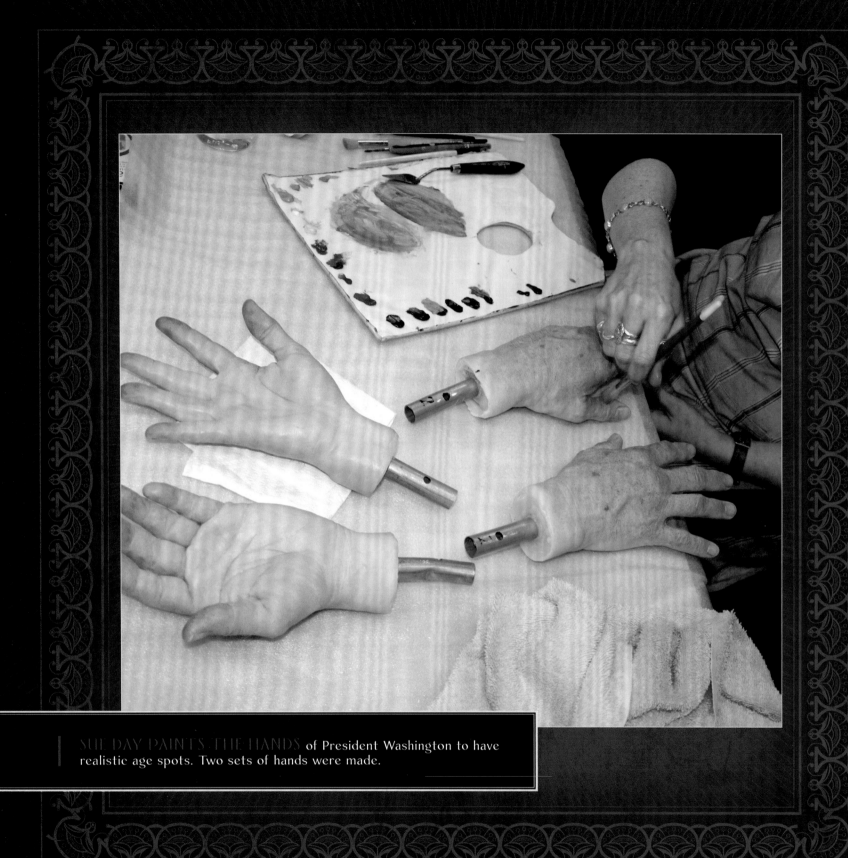

SUE DAY PAINTS THE HANDS of President Washington to have realistic age spots. Two sets of hands were made.

CHAPTER NINE

WASHINGTON AT FIFTY-SEVEN

Only one tooth remained in George Washington's mouth on the day he was inaugurated as the first president of the United States. That lone tooth and the denture that fit around it would prove invaluable in remaking his image more than two hundred years later.

THE FACE OF A NEW NATION

The Mount Vernon exhibit would portray President Washington as he placed his hand on the Bible, right before he opened his mouth to take the oath of office. When Stuart Williamson created the portrait sculpture of President Washington, his goal was to reflect on his face the "enormity of the moment." When he sculpted the face of the fifty-seven-year-old president, Williamson considered the Gilbert Stuart portraits of Washington. He also studied the faces of people today who have major tooth loss to show how Washington's tooth loss affected his face.

Williamson used his skill and knowledge of how gravity pulls on the fleshy areas of an aging face to create natural-looking hills and valleys of Washington's wrinkles. He sculpted in details like natural lip creases, a slightly raised vein on his right temple, and the smallpox scar on his left cheek. When Williamson was finished, he had captured in clay an expression on President Washington's face that reflects the dignity of his character as well as the emotion of the occasion.

When the wax head was ready, Williamson placed blue-gray eyeballs that had more red veining in them than the other two sets of eyes to reflect the eyes of an older man.

With her fifteen shades of paint, Sue Day created Washington's complexion, complete with tiny red blood vessels close to the surface of his skin. She painted his lips a natural color and used the perfect shade of light blue to paint the vein on his temple. Day took white plaster hands and transformed them with realistic age spots and blue veins. Then strand by strand, she placed hair on the back of his hands.

At fifty-seven, Washington had some gray in his reddish-brown hair. However, on formal occasions during the eighteenth century, fashionable gentlemen either wore a white wig or used white powder on their hair. Since Washington never wore a wig, his hair was powdered on Inauguration Day. The artists chose to use gray hair on the figure of President Washington to depict his powdered hair.

Day spent about five days inserting each gray hair into the wax head of President Washington—the same amount of time as it took to insert the hair for the other two. As she worked to get the hairline in the correct shape, she studied the hairlines of the other two figures and portraits of Washington. When she was done, each hair appeared to be growing naturally from his head. For his eyebrows, Day used a combination of gray and white hair, rather than the darker colors used when he was younger, and she made them thinner than before.

For President Washington's wig, Steven Horak knotted one gray hair at a time into the netting he custom fit to the back of Washington's wax head. The wig took twenty-four hours to complete. As planned, when Horak placed his wig on President Washington's head, it met perfectly with the hairline inserted by Day.

To style the hair of President Washington, Horak used a curling rod similar to the tools that would have been used in the eighteenth century. Horak heated the tool and carefully used it to curl the fragile gray hair above the ears—giving President Washington his familiar hairstyle. Horak used curlers in the back to give the

rest of Washington's hair an appropriate amount of wave. Next, he brushed the hair back in a queue and secured it in a small black silk bag with a bow at the top.

With the face and hands of President Washington completed, the last step was to re-create the inauguration clothes he wore as he stood on the balcony of Federal Hall.

INAUGURAL ATTIRE

Since the war interrupted trade between Great Britain and the American colonies, probably few Americans ordered clothing from British tailors as they had done before. By 1789 only a few locations in the United States had begun to manufacture cloth—and their early attempts produced cloth that was far inferior to that of British cloth. In January 1789, Washington asked his friend Henry Knox in New York to purchase some cloth for him from a manufacturer in Hartford, Connecticut. By March, Knox wrote Washington that he was informed that they would soon have available some "superfine brown Hartford cloth." When the company in Hartford found out that Washington wanted its best cloth, the company gave it to him at no charge "as A Token of their Respect & Esteem." The suit he wore during his inauguration was made from this cloth from Hartford.

To re-create President Washington's inaugural suit, Henry Cooke chose modern fabric that matched the color, the weight, and the style of the historic fabric. Sewing mostly by hand, Cooke matched the size of the garments exactly to the suits actually worn by Washington.

No detail was ignored. Eyewitness accounts of Washington's inauguration mentioned the buttons on Washington's suit had eagles on them. To re-create these buttons, Cooke hired Ken Wagner to fabricate brass buttons. On each button, Lynn Zelisnikar, an engraver at Colonial Williamsburg, engraved an eagle holding arrows in one talon and an olive branch in the other. Workers at Carousel Jewelry Clinic in Swansea, Massachusetts, covered the buttons in a thin layer of gold. Finally, Henry Cooke sewed the gleaming buttons in place on the suit.

Neal Hurst used tiny hand stitches and the highest-quality linen to make the shirt and stock worn by the figure of President Washington. He crafted the garments according to the latest fashion, which in 1789 included a slightly larger collar and wide, pleated ruffles down the front and at the sleeves.

The formal shoes worn by President Washington took Ken Treese twenty hours to make by hand. They were closed with stylish buckles. The white leg stockings—similar to those worn by matadors—came from Spain.

On his Inauguration Day, there was no question in the minds of the American people who the first president of the United States of America should be. The only choice was George Washington, the trusted, respected, and admired commander in chief of the Continental Army who fought for eight long years to gain independence from Britain. Throughout his life, he had consistently put the needs of his country over his own needs. The public knew he would continue to do so. Both the man and his new country would become world leaders.

PRESIDENT GEORGE WASHINGTON as he would have looked at the age of fifty-seven on his Inauguration Day, April 30, 1789

GEORGE WASHINGTON, surveyor, general, and president

CHAPTER TEN

THE REAL GEORGE WASHINGTON

The figures were complete, and once again, George Washington came home to his beloved Mount Vernon. The three dramatic life-size figures of Washington at the ages of nineteen, forty-five, and fifty-seven are the centerpieces of the Donald W. Reynolds Museum and Education Center. The entire project was made possible by a grant from the Donald W. Reynolds Foundation.

The team of experts who created them came from the fields of anthropology, science, technology, art history, and textiles. They were artists, scholars, tailors, taxidermists, and craftspeople of all sorts. Their efforts show that the study of human history is not confined to research libraries or archaeological digs. Our understanding of the past grows broader and deeper when we look at the past from a variety of perspectives. The expertise of each member of the team added to the body of knowledge about George Washington and the world in which he lived. They helped transform Washington and his world from a vague impression in visitors' minds to something they could see and appreciate.

In the past, visitors to Mount Vernon often thought of Washington only as the grumpy, boring image they knew from the Gilbert Stuart portrait and from the money in their pockets. Today's visitors leave with a very different vision of George Washington. Mount Vernon president James C. Rees says that the

new education center, and particularly the figures of George Washington, have helped us to convince people that Washington wasn't just the most powerful man of the period, but also the most fascinating. And because the exhibits focus on his youth as much as his later years, we're able to watch a free-spirited, wildly ambitious young man grow into the greatest leader our nation has ever known. His life reveals itself as one incredible adventure after another, and there's not a single boring chapter in the story. People now leave Mount Vernon feeling they know a far different man than the old man on the dollar bill, and that we were blessed that he accepted the challenge of fathering our country. People who respect Washington when they walk through the doors of Mount Vernon, but

don't really know him or like him, feel like they have gotten to really know him by the time they leave the estate. They really feel good about Washington, and that makes them feel good about America.

The three figures of George Washington help inform visitors about the personality, character, and leadership of the man. He was a strong, tall, handsome man who moved with natural athletic grace. He was always well-dressed and conducted himself with proper manners. He personally led his men into battle and was fearless in the face of danger. He was famous and yet was unaffected by admiration. He had personal integrity and the trust of the American public. He was chosen to command the war for independence and elected to be the first president of the new nation. He was an exciting man who became a remarkable leader—not because he wanted to be one but because it was his duty. This is the real George Washington.

A NOTE FROM THE AUTHOR

I love to watch the History Channel—no surprise since I write nonfiction about historical topics. One day, I watched a documentary titled *The Search for George Washington*. It showed how Mount Vernon brought together a team of experts from various fields to find out what George Washington really looked like. I was fascinated by the project, and the idea for the book you hold in your hands was born as I watched that documentary.

Just as re-creating George Washington took the cooperation and collaboration of dozens of talented individuals, the book I imagined would not have been possible without the assistance and generosity of a great many people.

I would like to thank the Donald W. Reynolds Foundation. Its generosity made the three representations of George Washington and the Donald W. Reynolds Museum and Education Center at George Washington's Mount Vernon Estate and Gardens a reality.

I am deeply grateful to the Mount Vernon Ladies' Association for preserving a vital piece of American history. Through the leadership of Mrs. Boyce Ansley and James Rees, Mount Vernon will continue to serve visitors for generations to come. This book would not have been possible without Mount Vernon's leadership and staff. From the beginning, Ann Bay, vice president for education, understood my vision for this book. Her knowledge about the creation of these figures was crucial to my research. I am especially grateful to Ann for allowing me to spend as much time as I needed at Mount Vernon. Each day I spent there was a delight and allowed me to better understand George Washington. My deepest appreciation goes to Diana Cordray, education center manager and special projects coordinator, for showing me the behind-the-scenes details of three Washington figures and helping me understand their construction. Her expertise, assistance, and generosity were invaluable to me throughout this project in ways too numerous to list. Diana and her husband, Dennis, showered me with hospitality and made my visits there feel as if I were at home. I owe a special thank-you to Mary V. Thompson, an extraordinary research historian with extensive knowledge of George Washington. Mary graciously answered many questions and supplied me with valuable source material. I appreciate the help of many others at Mount Vernon who have helped me in a variety of ways, including Dawn Bonner, Christina L. Keyser, Cal McWhirter, Jennifer Van Horn, Laura Simo, Sabrina Hiedemann, Yvonne Jones, Melissa Wood, Esther White, Stacey Stevens, Priscilla Osterhoudt, Dave Gaydos, Katie Pohlmann, Sonny Brinckman, and Joan Stahl.

My deep appreciation goes to Ivan Schwartz, Elliot Schwartz, and Debra Schwartz at StudioEIS. Ivan answered my questions, Elliot shared his photographs of the creative process as well as the incredible images of the finished figures, and Debra allowed me to visit the studio to see the artists' work.

A very special thank-you to Sue Day, Stuart Williamson, and Steven Horak, talented artists who I was privileged to watch work. They answered many questions with patience and kindness—thank you, dear friends.

I appreciate the help of Jeffrey Schwartz, departments of anthropology and history and philosophy of science, University of Pittsburgh, who shared his work with me.

Thank you to Anshuman Razdan, PRISM executive committee and associate engineering professor at Arizona State University, who provided me with information and images. I'd also like to thank the gifted and dedicated PRISM team: Matthew Tocheri, Scott Van Note, Jeremy Hansen, Dianne Hansford, Gene Cooper, Gerald Farin, and Dan Collins.

I deeply appreciate the assistance of Ellen Miles, curator of painting and sculpture at the Smithsonian National Portrait Gallery, who shared her knowledge and gave me a tour of the Washington portraits in the National Portrait Gallery.

I am grateful to Linda Baumgarten, curator of textiles and costumes at Colonial Williamsburg, for helping me understand eighteenth-century clothing. Others at the Colonial Williamsburg Foundation helped in important ways, including: Cathy Hellier, Ron Carnegie, Marianne Martin, and Penna Rogers.

Frank Zitz, thank you for sharing your work on Blueskin with me.

My admiration goes to the men and women who created the clothes worn by the three figures of Washington and the tack on Blueskin. I am grateful to each of them—Henry Cooke, Jim Kladder, Jay Howlett, Neal Hurst, Mark Hutter, Jimmy Leach, Stuart Lilie, Kenneth Treese, and Lynn Zelisniker— for explaining their work to me.

Thank you to the many others who shared their knowledge and expertise on a wide variety of topics: Rob Evans, who painted the exhibit murals; Arlene Shaner, assistant curator and reference librarian for historical collections, the New York Academy of Medicine; R. Scott Stephenson, the American Revolution Center; Scott Swank, the Dr. Samuel D. Harris National Museum of Dentistry; Brenda Baker and Craig Keeling at Arizona State University; Marie Birgitta, Kreylser and Associates; Jane Clark and Thomas A. Markwardt, Fort Necessity National Battlefield; Dona McDermott, Valley Forge National Historic Park; Louise West, who shared her family's story of the dental forceps with me; Eric Robinson and Jill Pazereckas, New York Historical Society; William C. Luebke and Dana Puga at the Library of Virginia; Michael Callahan, Federal Hall; Jennifer Patton and Suzanne Prabucki at Fraunces Tavern Museum; Debbie Vaughn at the Chicago History Museum; Susan Drinan, Atwater Kent Museum; Jude Pfister and Johnna-Lee Smith, Morristown National Historic Park; Alma Withers, Dave Muraca, Melanie Marquis, and Tabitha Hilliard at George Washington's Ferry Farm; the dig team at Ferry Farm: Bekah Sargeant, David Hazen, Teryn Goodman, Susan Young, Clint King, Jill Ficarrotta, Giselle Portuondo, Keri Sansevere, Mike Durkin, and Adrean Bastien; the dig team at Mount Vernon: Anne Beaubien, Susan Grealy, Alyssa Marizan, Courtney Williams, Kra Runkle, Jocelyn Brabyn, David Oder and Alana Newman; and Christina Hills.

I'd like to thank my agent, Susan Cohen, for her excellent guidance. My deepest appreciation goes to Andrew Karre, my editor at Carolrhoda, who shared my enthusiasm for this project and my vision for what this book could be. Thank you, Andrew and your talented team at Carolrhoda, for making the reality of this book even more beautiful than the one I'd imagined.

TIMELINE

1732   George Washington is born on February 22.

1743   Augustine Washington Sr., Washington's father, dies.

1749–1752   Washington works as a professional surveyor. The first figure now on display at Mount Vernon is of nineteen-year-old Washington surveying the American wilderness.

1752   Lawrence, Washington's half brother, dies. Washington's military career begins when he is appointed a major in the colonial militia.

1754   Washington is promoted to the rank of lieutenant colonel. He leads a surprise attack against a group of French soldiers. The skirmish marks the start of the French and Indian War (1754-1763).

1755   Washington serves as an aide to British Major General Edward Braddock during his campaign during the French and Indian War.

1759   Washington marries Martha Dandridge Custis.

1775   The American Revolution begins. Washington attends the Second Continental Congress in Philadelphia and is unanimously elected commander in chief of the Continental Army.

1776   The Declaration of Independence is written. Washington leads his army across the Delaware River and achieves his first major victory at Trenton, New Jersey.

1777–1778   Washington brings his troops through a harsh winter at Valley Forge, Pennsylvania. The figure of forty-five-year-old Washington depicts him during this period.

1781   Washington's army defeats Lord Charles Cornwallis in a decisive battle at Yorktown, Virginia. This is the last major battle of the American Revolution.

1783   The war ends when the United States and Great Britain sign a peace treaty.

1784–1787   Washington returns to Mount Vernon to retire from public life. He works to restore his property and business interests.

1785   French sculptor Jean-Antoine Houdon creates a clay bust and life mask of Washington's face to use in crafting a life-sized statue of the celebrated general.

1787   Washington presides over the Constitutional Convention in Philadelphia. He is the first man to sign the Constitution.

1788   Houdon completes his life-sized sculpture of Washington.

1789–1793   Washington is elected as the first president of the United States. The third figure at Mount Vernon depicts the fifty-seven-year-old at his Inauguration Day in April 1789.

1793–1797   Washington serves a second presidential term.

1796   Gilbert Stuart paints the portrait of Washington that appears on the dollar bill. Houdon's completed life-sized statue of Washington is placed in the Virginia capitol.

1797   Washington retires permanently to Mount Vernon.

1799   On December 14, Washington dies from illness.

SOURCE NOTES

5   John Neal, *Randolph, a Novel*, quoted in *Observations on American Art: Selections from the Writings of John Neal (1793–1876)* (State College: Pennsylvania State College, 1943), 2, 3.

6   "Anecdotical Recollections—No. III," *New Monthly Magazine and Literary Journal* 19 (London: Henry Colburn, 1827), 562–563.

6   Julian Ursyn Niemcewicz, *Under Their Vine and Fig Tree: Travels through America in 1797–1799, 1805 with Some Further Account of Life in New Jersey*, trans. and ed. with an introduction and notes by Metchie J. E. Budka (Newark, NJ: Grassman Publishing Company, 1965), 85.

6   Ibid., 84.

7   Lillian B. Miller, *Rembrandt Peale 1778–1860: A Life in the Arts, an Exhibition at the Historical Society of Pennsylvania* (Philadelphia: Historical Society of Pennsylvania, 1985), 32.

8   James Rees, personal communication with the author, June 21, 2010.

8–9   James Rees, personal communication with the author, August 24, 2010.

9   George Washington, letter to Henry Lee, July 2, 1792, The Papers of George Washington Digital Edition, The American Founding Era Collection (Charlottesville: University of Virginia Press, 2008), available online at http://rotunda .upress.virginia.edu/founders/ GEWN.html (November 1, 2010).

10   Jeffrey H. Schwartz, "Putting a Face on the First President," *Scientific American*, February 2006, 85.

13   David Humphreys, letter to George Washington, July 17, 1785, The Papers of George Washington.

14   George Washington, journal entry, October 10, 1785, The Papers of George Washington.

19   Mary V. Thompson, "Houdon's Bust of Washington," Mount Vernon Annual Report 2000, available online at http://www.mountvernon.org/ learn/collections/index.cfm/pid/238/ (August 23, 2010).

20   Anshuman Razdan, personal communication with the author, February 16, 2009.

22   Ibid.

25   George Washington, journal entry, March 15, 1748, The Papers of George Washington.

26   Thomas Jefferson, letter to Walter Jones, January 2, 1814, *The Writings of Thomas Jefferson*, vol. 14 (Washington, DC: Thomas Jefferson Memorial Association of the United States, 1903), 46.

28   George Washington, journal entry, November 22, 1753, The Papers of George Washington.

28   Legardeur de Saint-Pierre, letter to Robert Dinwiddie, December 15, 1753, The Papers of George Washington.

29   George Washington, journal entry, December 23, 1753, The Papers of George Washington.

31   Robert Dinwiddie, "Governor Dinwiddie's Instructions to Major Washington," quoted in George Washington, *Journal of Colonel George Washington Commanding a Detachment of Virginia Troops Sent by Robert Dinwiddie* (Albany, NY: Joel Munsell's Sons, 1893), 17.

32   George Washington, letter to John Augustine Washington, May 31, 1754, The Papers of George Washington.

34   George Washington, letter to unknown recipient, 1757, The Papers of George Washington.

35   David Humphreys, *David Humphreys' "Life of General Washington" with George Washington's "Remarks,"* ed.,

with an introduction, by Rosemarie Zagarri (Athens: University of Georgia Press, 1991), 15.

38   George Washington, letter to John Augustine Washington, July 18, 1755, The Papers of George Washington.

45   George Washington, letter to Charles Lawrence, April 26, 1763, The Papers of George Washington.

45–46   George Mercer, 1759, quoted in Albert Bushnell Hart, "Personal Appearance (1759–1799)," *Tributes to Washington*, pamphlet 3, pt. 1 (Washington, DC: George Washington Bicentennial Commission, 1931).

46   Linda Baumgarten, personal communication with the author, March 28, 2008.

48   Ivan Schwartz, personal communication with the author, November 12, 2008.

49   Stuart Williamson, personal communication with the author, August 24, 2010.

50   Ibid.

50   Ibid.

54   Sue Day, personal communication with the author, October 17, 2008.

58–59   George Washington, letter to George William Fairfax, May 31, 1775, The Papers of George Washington.

59   John Adams, letter to Abigail Adams, June 17, 1775, *Letters of Delegates to Congress, 1774–1789*, ed. Paul H. Smith, 26 vol. (Washington, DC: Library of Congress, 1976–2000), 498, available online at http:// memory.loc.gov/ammem/amlaw/ lwdg.html (November 23, 2010).

60   George Washington, letter to Martha Washington, June 18, 1775, The Papers of George Washington.

60   James Thacher, journal entry, July 20, 1775, *Eyewitness to the American*

Revolution: The Battles and Generals as Seen by an Army Surgeon (Stamford, CT: Longmeadow Press, 1994).

63-64 Henry Knox, letters to Lucy Knox, July 15, 1776, and July 22, 1776, quoted in Henry Steele Commager and Richard B. Morris, eds., *The Spirit of Seventy-Six: The Story of the American Revolution as Told by Its Participants* (New York: HarperCollins, 2002), 426–427.

65-66 Benjamin Tallmadge, *Memoir of Col. Benjamin Tallmadge, Prepared by Himself, at the Request of His Children* (New York: Thomas Holman, 1858), 11, 12.

66 David Ackerson, letter to his son, quoted in Henry Cabot Lodge, *George Washington*, vol. 2 (Boston: Houghton Mifflin, 1898), 386, 387.

68 Samuel Shaw, *The Journals of Major Samuel Shaw: The First American Consul at Canton* (Boston: Wm. Crosby and H. P. Nichols, 1847; repr., Bedford, MA: Applewood Books, 2009), 29, 30.

68 George Washington, general orders, December 27, 1776, The Papers of George Washington.

68 Robert Morris, letter to George Washington, January 1, 1777, The Papers of George Washington.

68 James Craik, letter to George Washington, January 6, 1778, The Papers of George Washington.

69 Tallmadge, *Memoir*, 25.

69 George Washington, letter to Patrick Henry, December 27, 1777, The Papers of George Washington.

70 George Washington, letter to George Clinton, February 16, 1778, The Papers of George Washington.

70 James Thacher, *Eyewitness*, 128.

70 Joseph Plumb Martin, *A Narrative of a Revolutionary Soldier: Some of the Adventures, Danger, and Sufferings of Joseph Plumb Martin* (New York: Signet, 2001), 89.

70–71 Pierre-Etienne Duponceau, letter to unknown recipient, quoted in Gilbert Chinard, ed. and trans., *George Washington as the French Knew Him: A Collection of Texts* (Princeton, NJ: Princeton University Press, 1940), 14.

78 Fred Hanson, "A Tailor Well-Suited for the Job," *Quincy (MA) Patriot Ledger*, August 5, 2006.

78 Henry Cooke, telephone conversation with author, August 10, 2009.

78–79 George Washington to Charles Lawrence, October 24, 1763, The Papers of George Washington.

79 George Washington to Charles Lawrence, June 20, 1768, The Papers of George Washington.

84–85 Marquis de Lafayette to George Washington Parke Custis, quoted in George Washington Parke Custis, *Recollections and Private Memories of Washington* (New York: Derby and Jackson, 1860), 220, 221.

85 Abbé Robin, letter to unknown recipient, quoted in Chinard, *George Washington as the French Knew Him*, 68, 69.

86–87 Martin, *A Narrative*, 200, 201.

87 Thacher, *Eyewitness*, 289.

88 Tallmadge, *Memoir*, 63.

88 Ibid.

89 Ibid., 64.

90 James Tilton to Gunning Bedford, December 25, 1783, quoted in John P. Kaminski and Jill Adair McCaughan, eds., *A Great and Good Man: George Washington in the Eyes of His Contemporaries* (Lanham, MD: Rowman & Littlefield Publishers, 1989), 26, 27.

90 George Washington, resignation address to the Continental Congress, December 23, 1783, The Papers of George Washington, available online at http://gwpapers.virginia.edu/documents/revolution/resignation.html (November 23, 2010).

93 George Washington, letter to James Madison, November 5, 1786, The Papers of George Washington.

93 Edmund Randolph, letter to George Washington, December 6, 1786, The Papers of George Washington.

93 George Washington, letter to Edmund Randolph, March 28, 1787, The Papers of George Washington.

94 Ibid.

95 George Washington, journal entry, September 17, 1787, The Papers of George Washington.

96 Humphreys, *David Humphreys'*, 47.

96 Ibid., 54.

96 Ibid., 50.

96–97 Charles Thompson, address to George Washington, April 14, 1789, The Papers of George Washington.

97 George Washington, journal entry, April 16, 1789, The Papers of George Washington.

98 U. S. Constitution, article 2, section 1.

99 I. N. Phelps Stokes, *The Iconography of Manhattan Island: 1498–1909: Compiled from Original Sources and Illustrated by Photo-Intaglio Reproductions of Important Maps, Plans, Views, and Documents in Public and Private Collections*, vol. 5 (New York: Robert H. Dodd, 1926; repr., New York: Arno Press, 1967), 1,244.

99 Ibid.

101 Stuart Williamson, personal communication with the author, November 12, 2008.

103 Henry Knox, letter to George Washington, March 5, 1789, The Papers of George Washington.

103 Daniel Hinsdale, letter to George Washington, March 23, 1789, The Papers of George Washington.

108 James Rees, personal communication with the author, September 13, 2010.

SELECTED BIBLIOGRAPHY

BOOKS

Barratt, Carrie Rebora, and Ellen G. Miles. *Gilbert Stuart.* Metropolitan Museum of Art series. New York: Metropolitan Museum of Art, 2004.

Baumgarten, Linda. *Eighteenth-Century Clothing at Williamsburg.* Williamsburg, VA: Colonial Williamsburg Foundation, 1986.

——. *What Clothes Reveal: The Language of Clothing in Colonial and Federal America.* Williamsburg, VA: Colonial Williamsburg Foundation, 2002.

Baumgarten, Linda, John Watson, and Florine Carr. *Costume Close-Up: Clothing Construction and Pattern 1750–1790.* Williamsburg, VA: Colonial Williamsburg Foundation, 1999.

Brady, Patricia. *Martha Washington: An American Life.* New York: Penguin, 2005.

Burda, Patricia, Ellen G. Miles, Cynthia J. Mills, and Leslie Kaye Reinhardt. *American Paintings of the Eighteenth Century.* The Collections of the National Gallery of Art: Systematic Catalogue series. New York: Oxford University Press, 1995.

Butterfield, L. H., Marc Friedlaender, and Mary-Jo Kline, eds. *The Book of Abigail and John: Selected Letters of the Adams Family 1762–1784.* Cambridge, MA: Harvard University Press, 89, 100.

Cadou, Carol. *The George Washington Collection: Fine and Decorative Arts at Mount Vernon.* Manchester, VT: Hudson Hills Press, 2006.

Carson, Jane. *We Were There: Descriptions of Williamsburg 1699–1859 Compiled from Contemporary Sources and Arranged Chronologically.* Williamsburg, VA: Colonial Williamsburg Foundation, 1965.

Chinard, Gilbert, ed. and trans. *George Washington as the French Knew Him: A Collection of Texts.* Princeton, NJ: Princeton University Press, 1940.

Commager, Henry Steele, and Richard B. Morris, eds. *The Spirit of Seventy-Six: The Story of the American Revolution as Told by Its Participants.* New York: Da Capo Press, 1995.

Custis, George Washington Parke. *Recollections and Private Memoirs of Washington.* New York: Derby & Jackson, 1860.

Ellis, Joseph J. *His Excellency George Washington.* New York: Alfred Knopf, 2004.

Flexner, James Thomas. *George Washington and the New Nation (1783–1793).* Boston: Little, Brown, 1972.

——. *George Washington Anguish and Farewell (1793–1799).* Boston: Little, Brown, 1970.

——. *George Washington in the American Revolution (1775–1783).* Boston: Little, Brown, 1968.

——. *George Washington: The Forge of Experience (1732–1775).* Boston: Little, Brown, 1965.

——. *Washington: The Indispensable Man.* Boston: Little, Brown, 1974.

Garrett, Wendell, ed. *George Washington's Mount Vernon.* New York: Monacelli Press, 1998.

Henriques, Peter R. *Realistic Visionary: A Portrait of George Washington.* Charlottesville: University of Virginia Press, 2006.

Hevner, Carol Eaton, ed. With a biographical essay by Lillian B. Miller. *Rembrandt Peale 1778–1860 A Life in the Arts, an Exhibition at the Historical Society of Pennsylvania.* Philadelphia: Historical Society of Pennsylvania, 1985.

Humphreys, David. *David Humphreys' "Life of General Washington" with George Washington's "Remarks."* Edited with an introduction by Rosemarie Zagarri. Athens: University of Georgia Press, 1991.

Kaminski, John P., and Jill Adair McCaughan, eds. *A Great and Good Man: George Washington in the Eyes of his Contemporaries.* Lanham, MD: Rowman & Littlefield Publishers, 1989.

Keller, Kate Van Winkle, and Charles Cyril Hendrickson. *George Washington: A Biography in Social Dance.* Sandy Hook, CT: Hendrickson Group, 1998.

Lengel, Edward G. *This Glorious Struggle: George Washington's Revolutionary War Letters.* New York: Collins, 2007.

Martin, Joseph Plumb. *A Narrative of a Revolutionary Soldier: Some of the Adventures, Danger, and Sufferings of Joseph Plumb Martin.* New York: Signet, 2001.

Miles, Ellen G. *American Paintings of the Eighteenth Century.* Washington, DC: National Gallery of Art, 1995.

Mount, Charles Merrill. *Gilbert Stuart: A Biography.* New York: Norton, 1964.

Mount Vernon Official Guidebook. Mount Vernon, VA: Mount Vernon Ladies' Association, n.d.

Niemcewicz, Julian Ursyn. *Under Their Vine and Fig Tree: Travels through America in 1797–1799, 1805 with Some Further Account of Life in New Jersey.* Translated by Metchie J. E. Budka. Newark, NJ: Grasssman Publishing Company, 1965.

Olmert, Michael, Suzanne E. Coffman, and Paul Aron. *Official Guide to Colonial Williamsburg.* Williamsburg, VA: Colonial Williamsburg Foundation, 2007.

Rhodehamel, John, ed. *George Washington Writings.* New York: Library of America, 1997.

Ribblett, David L. *Nelly Custis: Child of Mount Vernon.* Mount Vernon, VA: Mount Vernon Ladies' Association, 1993.

Schecter, Barnet. *The Battle for New York: The City at the Heart of the Revolution.* New York: Penguin, 2002.

Shaw, Samuel. *The Journal of Major Samuel Shaw: The First American Consul at Canton.* Boston: Wm. Crosby and H. P. Nichols, 1847; Reprint. Bedford, MA: Applewood Books, 2009.

Tallmadge, Benjamin. *Memoir of Col. Benjamin Tallmadge, Prepared by Himself, at the Request of His Children.* New York: Thomas Holman, 1858.

Thacher, James. *Eyewitness to the American Revolution: The Battles and Generals as Seen by an Army Surgeon.* Stamford, CT: Longmeadow Press, 1994.

Thompson, Mary V. *In the Hand of a Good Providence: Religion in the Life of George Washington.* Charlottesville: University of Virginia Press, 2008.

Von Steuben, Frederick William Baron. *Baron von Steuben's Revolutionary War Drill Manual: A Facsimile Reprint of the 1794 Edition.* New York: Dover Publications. 1985.

Washington, George. *Journal of Colonel George Washington, Commanding a Detachment of Virginia Troops Sent by Robert Dinwiddie, Lieutenant-Governor of Virginia, across the Alleghany Mountains, in 1754.* Edited with notes by J. M. Toner. Albany, NY: Joel Munsell's Sons, 1893.

——. *Revolutionary War Letters: This Glorious Struggle.* Edited by Edward Lengel. Washington, DC: Smithsonian Books, 2007.

——. *Rules of Civility and Decent Behaviour in Company and Conversation.* Bedford, MA: Applewood Books, 1988.

ARTICLES AND PRIMARY SOURCE DOCUMENTS

Brookes, Joshua. "A Dinner at Mount Vernon: From the Unpublished Journal of Joshua Brookes (1773–1859)." Edited by R. W. G. Vail. *New York Historical Society Quarterly* 31, no. 2 (April 1947): 75–76.

Gist, Christopher. *Journal of Christopher Gist.* USGenWeb Archives Pennsylvania. N.d. http://www.usgwarchives.net/pa/1pa/1picts/gist/gj3b.html (July 10, 2008).

GPO. "George Washington." Catalogue of Fine Art. GPO Access. 2009. http://www.gpoaccess.gov/serialset/cdocuments/sd107-11/pdf/386-413.pdf (January 5, 2009).

Miles, Ellen G. "Presidential Portraits." *Colonial Williamsburg Journal,* Spring 2007. Available online at http://m.history.org/Foundation/journal/Spring07/portraits.cfm (March 18, 2010).

Mount Vernon Ladies' Association. George Washington's Mount Vernon Estate and Gardens Collections. N.d. http://www.mountvernon.org/learn/collections/index.cfm (April 14, 2009).

Peale, Rembrandt. *Washington and His Portraits*. Smithsonian Archives of American Art, Rembrandt and Harriet Peale Papers, 1824-1832. N.d. http://www.aaa.si.edu/collectionsonline/pealremb/container137443.htm (May 26, 2010).

Redmond, Edward. "George Washington: Surveyor and Mapmaker." Library of Congress. N.d. http://memory.loc.gov/ammem/gmdhtml/gwmaps.html (May 24, 2008).

Thompson, Mary V. "That Hospitable Mansion: Hospitality at George Washington's Mount Vernon." George Washington's Mount Vernon Estate and Gardens. 2010. http://www.mountvernon.org/pdf/Foodways-Hospitality11.pdf (November 13, 2010).

University of Virginia Papers of George Washington. "George Washington's Resignation Address to the Continental Congress, Annapolis, Maryland, 23 December 1783." N.d. http://gwpapers.virginia.edu/documents/revolution/resignation.html (July 22, 2009).

U.S. Department of State. "State House, Annapolis, Nov. 26, 1793–Aug. 19, 1784." Office of the Historian. N.d. http://history.state.gov/departmenthistory/buildings/section9 (July 22, 2009).

Washington, George. The Papers of George Washington. University of Virginia. N.d. http://gwpapers.virginia.edu/documents/revolution/resignation.html (July 22, 2009).

———. *Surveying for Lord Fairfax 11 March–13 April 1748*. The Diaries of George Washington. Vol. 1. Edited by Donald Jackson and Dorothy Twohig. The Papers of George Washington. Charlottesville: University Press of Virginia, 1976. http://memory.loc.gov/cgi-bin/query/r?ammem/mgw:@field(DOCID+@lit(wd018)) (August 25, 2009).

THESIS

Hyson, J. M., Jr. "George Washington's Dental History and Relics." Masters thesis. Newark: University of Delaware, 1999.

DVD

The Search for George Washington. DVD. New York: History Channel, 2007.

Williamson, Stuart. *Portrait Sculpture: From the Inside Out*. DVD. Privately produced, 2009.

INTERVIEWS

Bay, Ann. Personal communication, e-mails, various dates, 2008–2010.

Cooke, Henry. Personal communication, e-mails, various dates, 2008–2010.

Cordray, Diana. Personal communication, e-mails, various dates, 2008–2010.

Day, Sue. Personal communication, e-mails, various dates, 2008–2010.

Evans, Rob. E-mail, February 2009.

Hellier, Cathy. Personal communication, e-mails, various dates, 2009–2010.

Horak, Steven. Personal communication, e-mails, various dates, 2008–2010.

Howlett, Jay. E-mails, August 2009.

Hurst, Neal. E-mails, September 2009.

Hutter, Mark. E-mails, September 2009.

Kladder, Jim. Personal communication, e-mails, various dates, 2009–2010.

Miles, Ellen. Personal communication, e-mails, various dates, 2008–2010.

Rees, James. E-mails, various dates, 2010.

Schwartz, Elliot. Personal communication, e-mails, various dates, 2009–2010.

Schwartz, Ivan. Personal communication, e-mails, various dates, 2008–2010.

Schwartz, Jeffrey. Personal communication, e-mails, various dates, 2008–2010.

Treese, Ken. E-mails, August 2009.

Williamson, Stuart. Personal communication, e-mails, various dates, 2008–2010.

FURTHER READING

BOOKS

Allen, Thomas B. *George Washington, Spymaster: How the Americans Outspied the British and Won the Revolutionary War.* Washington, DC: National Geographic, 2007.

Beller, Susan Provost. *Yankee Doodle and the Redcoats: Soldiering in the Revolutionary War.* Minneapolis: Twenty-First Century Books, 2008.

Freedman, Russell. *Lafayette and the American Revolution.* New York: Holiday House, 2010.

——. *Washington at Valley Forge.* New York: Holiday House, 2008.

Miller, Brandon Marie. *Declaring Independence: Life during the Revolutionary War.* Minneapolis: Twenty-First Century Books, 2005.

Murphy, Jim. *The Crossing: How George Washington Saved the American Revolution.* New York: Scholastic Press, 2010.

Walker, Sally M. *Written in Bone: Buried Lives of Jamestown and Colonial Maryland.* Minneapolis: Carolrhoda Books, 2009.

WEBSITES

Colonial Williamsburg
http://www.colonialwilliamsburg.com

Fort Necessity National Battlefield
http://www.nps.gov/fone/index.htm

Fraunces Tavern
http://www.frauncestavernmuseum.org/index.html

George Washington's Birthplace
http://www.nps.gov/gewa/index.htm

George Washington's Ferry Farm
http://www.kenmore.org/ff_home.html

George Washington's Mount Vernon Estate and Gardens
http://www.mountvernon.org

Morristown National Historic Park
http://www.nps.gov/morr/index.htm

Valley Forge National Historic Park
http://www.nps.gov/vafo/historyculture/index.htm

The Virginia State Capital, Visitors Guide
http://hodcap.state.va.us/publications/08_visitors_guide.pdf

Washington Crossing Historic Park
http://www.ushistory.org/washingtoncrossing/index.htm

Yorktown National Historic Park
http://www.nps.gov/york/index.htm

LERNER SOURCE

Expand learning beyond the printed book. Download free, complementary educational resources for this book from our website, www.lernerresource.com.

INDEX

PHOTO ACKNOWLEDGMENTS

The images in this book are used with the permission of: Gilbert Stuart, American, 1755–1828, *George Washington*, 1796, Oil on canvas, 121.28 x 93.98 cm (47 3/4 x 37 in.), Museum of Fine Arts, Boston, William Francis Warden Fund, John H. and Ernestine A. Payne Fund, Commonwealth Cultural Preservation Trust. Jointly owned by the Museum of Fine Arts, Boston, and the National Portrait Gallery, Washington D.C., 1980.1. Licensed by National Portrait Gallery, Smithsonian Institution/Art Resource, NY, p. 4; © iStockphoto.com/Steve Debenport, p. 6; Courtesy of the Philadelphia History Museum at the Atwater Kent, The Historical Society of Pennsylvania Collection, p. 7 (top); © Collection of the New-York Historical Society, USA/ The Bridgeman Art Library, p. 7 (bottom); Gilbert Stuart, *George Washington (Vaughan portrait)*, Andrew W. Mellon Collection, Image courtesy of the Board of Trustees, National Gallery of Art, Washington, p. 8 (left); Private collection/ Photo © Christie's Images/The Bridgeman Art Library, p. 8 (center); © Massachusetts Historical Society, Boston, MA, USA/ The Bridgeman Art Library, p. 8 (right); Colonial Williamsburg Foundation, pp. 9 (left), 31; *George Washington*, William Joseph Williams (1759-1823), Pastel on paper, 1794, 71.1 x 55.8 cm (28 x 22 in.), Property of Alexandria-Washington Lodge No. 22, Ancient, Free, and Accepted Masons, Alexandria, Virginia, Photography by Arthur W. Pierson, Falls Church, Virginia, p. 9 (right); Courtesy of Mount Vernon Ladies' Association, pp. 15, 32, 40 (bottom left), 57, 83, 86, 94, 105; Life Mask of George Washington, full face front view, Virginia, 1785, plaster, The Pierpont Morgan Library/Art Resource, NY, p. 16; The Library of Virginia, p. 17; Dr. Anshuman Razdan, Arizona State University, pp. 19, 20, 21 (both), 42, 43, 45; Library of Congress, pp. 24, 97 (LC-USZC4-7831); © Jeffrey M. Frank/ Shutterstock Images, p. 33; Tom Markwardt, Fort Necessity National Battlefield, National Park Service, p. 37; Courtesy of the National Museum of Dentistry, Baltimore, MD, p. 40 (top left and bottom right); Courtesy of the New York Academy of Medicine Library, pp. 40 (top right), 41; Kreysler & Associates, p. 47; Sculpture by StudioEIS, Brooklyn, NY, photo by Elliot Schwartz, pp. 48 (both), 49, 50, 55, 73, 106; Courtesy of author, Carla Killough McClafferty, pp. 53 (top left, top right, bottom left), 63, 74 (top), 91, 100, 103; © Cal McWhirter, pp. 53 (bottom right), 77; © Image Asset Management Ltd./SuperStock, p. 59; Courtesy of the American Revolution Center, p. 61; Peale, Charles Willson (1741-1827), *George Washington* (detail), ca. 1779-1781, oil on canvas, 95 x 61 3/4 in. (241.3 x 156.8 cm), Gift of Collis P. Huntington, 1897 (97.33), The Metropolitan Museum of Art, New York, NY, U.S.A. Image copyright © The Metropolitan Museum of Art/Art Resource, NY, p. 67 (left); Military History, National Museum of American History, Smithsonian Institution, pp. 67 (right), 80; © Diana Cordray, p. 74 (bottom); Dominic Quintana for Fraunces Tavern® Museum, p. 89; National Archives, pp. 95, 99.

Cover: Sculpture by StudioEIS, Brooklyn, NY, Photo by Elliot Schwartz (main); © Todd Strand/Independent Picture Service (top left); © The Bridgeman Art Library/Getty Images (top center); © Art Resource, NY (top right); © Eric Van Den Brulle/ Riser/Getty Images (bottom right).